Anxious in Love

Say Goodbye to Anxiety in Relationships. If I Can do it, YOU Can Too!

Amanda Palermo

Understanding and Overcoming Anxiety in Relationships. How to Stop and Overcome Couple Conflicts, Insecurity, and Jealousy, and Eliminate Negative Thinking to Build and Maintain a Healthy and Happy Relationship

© Copyright 2020 – Amanda Palermo. All rights reserved.

The contents of this book may not be reproduced, duplicated or transmitted without direct written permission from the author.

Under no circumstances will any legal responsibility or blame be held against the publisher for any reparation, damages, or monetary loss due to the information herein, either directly or indirectly.

Legal Notice:

This book is copyright protected. This is only for personal use. You cannot amend, distribute, sell, use, quote or paraphrase any part or the content within this book without the consent of the author.

Disclaimer Notice:

Please note the information contained within this document is for educational and entertainment purposes only. Every attempt has been made to provide accurate, up to date and reliable complete information. No warranties of any kind are expressed or implied. Readers acknowledge that the author is not engaging in the rendering of legal, financial, medical or professional advice. The content of this book has been derived from various sources. Please consult a licensed professional before attempting any techniques outlined in this book.

By reading this document, the reader agrees that under no circumstances is the author responsible for any losses, direct or indirect, which are incurred as a result of the use of information contained within this document, including, but not limited to, —errors, omissions, or inaccuracies.

Table of Contents

Introduction 5

Understanding Relationship Anxiety 13

Managing Relationship Anxiety - Acknowledgement, Negativity, and Jealousy 40

Managing Relationship Anxiety - Healthy Boundaries, Couple Conflicts, and Insecurity 63

Managing Your Inner Critic 86

Understanding Attachment Styles 109

Harnessing the Power of Positivity 126

Importance of Communication in Relationships 146

Self-Esteem and Self-Confidence in Relationships 160

Conclusion 177

References 183

Introduction

There was a time in my life when I enjoyed being myself and loved doing things on my own. Slowly, as I watched my friends get into great relationships, the need to have an intimate physical and emotional connection with another human being took seed in my heart and mind. Of course, this need to connect is a natural human instinct that none of us can escape from.

I can never forget my first wholesome romantic relationship. Both of us were young and totally in love. Romance powered our relationship beautifully. We were a 'perfect' couple watching old Meg Ryan movies cozily ever so often, hugging and kissing each other at the right moments, saying nice things, and complimenting each other as often as we could! Everything was unblemished and beautiful. Oh! It was a dream, and I felt this dream would go on forever.

But stupid, anxious me wouldn't allow the dream to go on forever! I ruined everything one forgettable evening when things got totally out of hand. He left me alone at home, saying that he needed to go for dinner with his colleagues from the law firm. I didn't believe him, thanks to my anxiety issues.

I thought he was lying to me and was secretly meeting Lidia, one of his co-workers. I always found this Lidia quite annoying. She would smirk and strut around with her huge bobbing boobs wearing heels that were nearly half a meter in height! That she had perfect thighs that looked like a cross between a spinning instructor and an anorexic model from Eastern Europe didn't help my own anxiety issues.

Driven by these worries, that fateful night, I followed him to the bar where he usually meets colleagues. It was raining cats and dogs, and I tried hard not to get wet and not to get caught. Of course, I got caught and made a complete fool of myself. After all, I hadn't been to Quantico and learned to follow without being seen.

Worse still, his colleagues started mocking him. They said nasty things like he was a prisoner in my clutches, and I followed him everywhere. They even said that maybe I had hired a private investigator to tail him, bug his car, or take pictures of him. That did it. He started seeing me with different eyes, and it was the beginning of my anxiety-driven downfall.

I have so many stories of my own life that I could write an epic on relationship anxiety. Therefore, I thought it would be a great idea to start every chapter in this book with an anecdote from my life, hoping

Introduction

you will learn the lesson through my painful (many times, funny too) experiences.

It is true that each of us is complete by ourselves. In theory, we don't need anyone outside of us to make us feel good and happy. It is true we make our own happiness, and we are responsible for our lives, and another person in our life only brings unnecessary complications. There is hardly a reason to refute these claims, at least theoretically.

However, in practical life, living alone is for hermits. Human beings are social animals, and we are lost when we are alone. We all need other human beings to share our joys and sorrows. And that is why relationships exist! Of all the types of relationships, the romantic kind is by far the most exciting, adventurous, and has the power to give us a huge high.

A great boyfriend, spouse, or partner adds immense value to your life. Being in a romantic relationship makes your day looks brighter, you feel wanted, loved, and desired, and you are filled with a sense of positivity that no other kind of relationship can make you feel. Being in a committed relationship has multiple benefits that only get better in the long-run.

You become more 'giving' - In a romantic relationship, we tend to give as much as we can to make our partner feel happy and good. As you practice the art of giving, you acquire the habit of giving. Also, your ability to share and feel love towards others improve significantly.

You learn to manage your expectations - Another important lesson you learn while in a committed, meaningful relationship is to keep your expectations at a reasonable, both from yourself as well as from others. You learn to do things for the sake of doing them and because you love doing them, and not because you expect something in return.

You feel a sense of belonging - You feel a deep sense of joy that comes with being in a stable, committed relationship. You know that no matter what, your relationship will endure, and that sense of certainty gives you meaning and purpose in your life. You get a feeling of belonging and connection with your partner.

And finally, of course, you feel that your partner belongs to you too. This interconnection between two human beings is a powerful element of life from which we draw inspiration and motivation to become better individuals even as we add value to our relationships.

Introduction

And yet, these very same elements of beauty and pleasure inherent to relationships can become the cause of relationship anxiety for some of us. Relationships can be a breeding ground for stress, anxiety, and worry. Anxiety in romantic relationships can erode our self-confidence and self-esteem. It can make us feel unworthy and undeserving of love. Being anxious in relationships is a common occurrence during the initial dating stages. We worry whether our potential partner will meet our expectations and/or worry whether we will meet the expectations of him or her.

Most first dates are filled with fear and anxiety as each of the two partners tries hard to please each other. The undercurrents of anxiety in the initial stages of a romantic relationship generally last for a couple of dates. However, this is not cast in stone.

Strangely and interestingly, relationship anxiety can happen at any stage of a relationship. So, already explained, you could feel anxious on your first date. But, you could also feel anxious in a relationship that has lasted for years! In fact, for some of us, the closer we get to our partner, the more anxious we become. For some others, the very idea of getting into a relationship can cause anxiety.

Short-term relationship anxiety might be a good thing because it keeps us on our toes and ensures that we work committedly towards making a success of our relationship. However, beyond a certain point, relationship anxiety is not good at all.

It can make us feel lonely and desolate and drive us away, not only from our current partner, but from the all-important human need of love itself. Learning about and understanding the causes and effects of relationship anxiety is a critical step in overcoming its negative effects. Read on to find out more about relationship anxiety and what you can do to prevent it from consuming your life.

Why should you read on? Who am I to give you advice on relationship anxiety? Well, I want to tell you that the contents of this book are based entirely on my personal experiences. Relationship anxiety had taken a big toll on my life.

After an agonizingly, painful, failed romance, I was so caught up in the anxiety caused by the pain of my boyfriend leaving me that I went adrift in ways that are not pleasant at all. I took to drugs not to mention had numerous one-night stands resulting in so many horrid and highly forgettable physical, mental, and emotional consequences that my loved ones thought my life was over.

Introduction

But I had one dedicated family member who trusted and believed in my ability to bounce back. She never gave up. She and I would have long conversations, many times in the middle of the night. We went traveling, and in each of these travels, she made sure I read up and learned about relationship anxiety and how easy it is actually to overcome it.

She taught me the importance of building self-awareness, self-confidence, self-esteem, and more. She showed me the path, and although she couldn't be there throughout my recovery process (she had a great life of her own), she ensured the path was lit at regular intervals, so I don't get lost.

Yes, I also got professional help to understand and overcome relationship anxiety. After six months of hard, committed, and dedicated work, my life was back on track. Today, it is easy for me to understand and read people and also know that works and doesn't work for me. Using my lessons, I have gained the confidence to trust in love and romance again and feel no pressure to get into relationships. And yet, when I know something has the potential to work, I don't hold back and give it my best efforts.

This book is a collection of all my personal lessons organized in a way that makes it easy for people like you to learn from and implement in your own lives. I hope you can use the lessons in this book as much as I used them to overcome relationship anxiety and discover love again.

Chapter One:

Understanding Relationship Anxiety

The next story I would like to tell you about my personal life deals with a lesson about how simple, minor, and easily-solvable differences in relationships, if left unresolved, have the power to jeopardize your relationships.

My partner and I had a minor difference. And because I (maybe both of us together) let this minor take control of our relationship, I lost out on an opportunity to create a fulfilling and meaningful love life for myself. Moreover, the pain from the collapse of this relationship left an indelible mark on my psyche, thereby enhancing my relationship anxiety more than I could handle on my own.

Let me give you more details. Earlier, I had already been dumped by a partner because of a silly difference, namely the love/hate for baseball. He loved baseball, and I hated it. I just couldn't understand how anyone could even watch the game, let alone go crazy about it.

Anxious in Love

How does one even begin to like a game that is as boring as spending an entire day watching people throw balls at each other so that someone could hit it and then someone else could catch it and return it to the place where it all began? I always thought baseball was a perfect example of running around in circles, not knowing where anyone was going at any point in time. Wouldn't it be better to play this kind of ball game with your dog in the park, and that too for free?

And do you even know how many baseball games take place every year in the country? I am sure there are more baseball games in the US than the number of hours in a year! And here I was with a boyfriend who thought that this game was the game of all games. He lived and breathed baseball. And thanks to the large number of games happening everywhere, his weekends will always work for baseball, regardless of what I wanted to do. For all practical purposes, I was non-existent when it comes to choosing between spending time with me or going for a game with his friends, either to play or to watch.

Maybe he was looking for someone who had a better connection to sports than I could ever have. Whatever was the reason, I caught him one day in bed with a softball player. The pain of being cheated on by your partner is so excruciating that the only way

Understanding Relationship Anxiety

anyone can understand it is by experiencing it. I certainly hope you don't have to experience that awful agony.

Anyway, that relationship ended with that scene of finding my boyfriend with the softball player, though later on, I learned that she was a park bench hoping she will fill in where and when I failed for him. I gave a whoop of joy when I heard this gossip. It made me feel good that he got what he deserved. The relationship ended, but the pain and mistrust endured for a long, long time affecting my relationship anxiety quite badly.

So, here I was, in a new relationship with another partner (I am going to call him Cullen) who loved classical music which I sort of hate, or perhaps, even never bothered to understand. I was more of the rock music type, especially of the 80s rock music. My favorite pastime was to listen to Bon Jovi, and his favorite was to listen to Beethoven's symphonies.

You can only imagine the noise that was created when the two of us chose to listen to our favorites simultaneously, just to get back at each other. We would not even use our headphones. We would only use two separate rooms in the house! The neighbors might have gone bonkers with it. It's a miracle they didn't report us. Or maybe there were busy solving their own problems and didn't care what happened elsewhere.

Jokes aside! The mistrust gained from my earlier relationship ensured that every time my partner was not with me, I imagined him making out or whispering sweet-nothings to a beautiful violinist even as they practice the notes of Verdi's Aida together. The green monster did not let me sleep in peace, and in turn, I didn't bother to resolve the minor difference in our liking for music. Instead, I allowed jealousy to creep in and destroy something that had the potential for greatness and everlasting beauty.

Now, in retrospect, I realize how easy it was to solve this minor difference between Cullen and me. All both of us had to do was take turns to listen to both kinds of music so that we develop an appreciation of both. After all, music is a universal power that can bring two hearts together. And here, we used it to break us apart because of earlier experiences.

One day, after a particularly bad day at the office, thanks to a nasty boss who screwed me for every small mistake I did, I returned home. There, I saw Cullen deeply involved as the music from one of his favorite classical music albums played in the background. I was already angry and frustrated because of the unpleasant day at the office.

I wanted to listen to some rock music so that I could dance away my blues, and here Cullen listening to some slow, boring music that only added to my frustration. Moreover, he didn't even look up and acknowledge my presence. He could see how tired and harried I was, right?

I wanted to get back at Cullen's indifferent behavior. He was sitting in the living room space. So, I put on loud rock music and started dancing away in the bedroom. Of course, rock music is a wee bit louder than classical music. Well, it is also true some of the crescendos in classical music can break glass, and Cullen knew that. So, he had no right to complain about the loudness of rock music.

He started screaming at me to lower the volume, and I screamed back at him to go somewhere else to listen to his classical music. One thing led to another, and he walked out that day and did not return at night. He came back after a couple of days, packed his bags, and went out without a single word exchanged between us. Actually, it was a tame way to end a good relationship. But both of us were too busy and caught up in our own likes and dislikes that we didn't have space, time, or energy for each other.

So, what really is relationship anxiety? It is the feelings of worry and insecurity that keep plaguing people even when they are in perfectly happy and engaging relationships. Suppose you are in a relationship with a person whom you love and admire greatly. Things are going fine between the two of you. There is trust in each other, you have established clear and healthy boundaries for your individual needs, and there is nothing to cause worry.

And yet, your mind is not at rest. You are continually questioning your relationships, your partner, and yourself. Questions like the following nag you constantly:

- Will this last?

- How do I know he or she will not leave me?

- What if he or she doesn't really love me?

- How do I know that this person is the perfect one for me?

The next question that needs to be addressed right now is, "If I have relationship anxiety, am I abnormal?" Well, the answer to this is, 'No, you are not!" It is perfectly natural to experience anxious thoughts, especially in romantic relationships considering that there is so much pressure on it in modern times. In fact, according to psychological experts, relationship anxiety is quite common.

Relationship anxiety can set in at any time. For some, it could be at the start of a new relationship. For others, relationship anxiety could be experienced before they know that their partner is equally interested in taking the relationship forward.

Some might be impacted by relationship anxiety so much that they might not even be sure if they want to commit to any kind of long-term relationship. Also, relationship anxiety can also be manifested in long-term, sustained relationships as well.

Most of us feel a little bit insecure about our relationships, especially before the time both partners commit to each other. These feelings are normal, and there is no need to worry excessively about them. However, if relationship anxiety creeps into your daily life and affects your normal functioning, then you need to do something about it.

Because if relationship anxiety is left unresolved then, over time, it can lead to multiple complications and problems including:

- Lack of motivation

- Emotional distress

- Emotional exhaustion

- Physical health issues like recurring headaches, stomachaches, physical tiredness, etc.

It is also important to note that your anxiety may not be caused by your partner or something in your relationship. However, unresolved anxiety issues can drive behaviors and attitudes, which lead to relationship problems.

Signs of Relationship Anxiety

Relationship anxiety manifests itself in many ways. Let us look at some of the common signs and symptoms here.

Always worrying about your value in the relationship - One of the most common questions many of us with relationship anxiety connect with is, "Do I matter to my partner and our relationship?"

At a very basic level, psychologists opine that this question reflects the fundamental human need to feel connected with other human beings. But, if and when this question reaches the depths of your being and prevents you from leading a happy life with your partner, then you could be feeling the effects of relationship anxiety.

Understanding Relationship Anxiety

Doubting your partner's feelings for you - Your partner is one of the most loving people you have come across. He or she has confessed his or her love for you multiple times and in numerous different ways, including repeating 'I love you' many times.

And yet, you don't seem satisfied and worry, "Does my partner really love me?" This doubt could come up because once they had been a little slow in responding to you. Perhaps, your partner was busy with work or had something at the office that kept him or her preoccupied.

But, you cannot stop that gnawing thought, "My partner doesn't seem to care for or love me anymore?" This kind of relentless worry and doubt about your partner's feelings for you could be a sign of relationship anxiety.

Worrying that your partner wants to break up - All of us feel loved, wanted, and secure in a great relationship. And it is perfectly natural to want to hold on to these feelings forever. It is natural to fear that something can disrupt a fabulous relationship, and it is also okay when you do things in the hope of keeping disruption out of your life.

Yet, when these kinds of thoughts persist to the point that you find it difficult to speak to your partner about real issues that need to be discussed, then there is a problem. For example, you could adjust your behavior to suit the needs of your partner so that they don't have a reason to leave you.

For example, you might choose not to bring up the issue of your partner coming home late from the office every day because you think he or she is uncomfortable answering your questions, or that he or she might perceive you as being controlling. Or, you are furious at your partner for something he or she did despite repeated reminders, say, for example, wearing shoes inside the house, a thing you don't like at all and have told your partner many times. But, you might hide your anger because you want to secure your partner's affection.

Worrying about long-term compatibility - Relationship anxiety could make you doubt whether you and/or your partner are capable of sustaining the relationship in the long-term horizon. You could believe romantic gestures and the exchange of gifts could serve their purpose in the short term.

However, the minute you think long-term, you might begin to doubt your compatibility quotient and its ability to take the relationship far into the future. In the same context, you could doubt your present state of happiness in the relationship. You could be

Understanding Relationship Anxiety

asking yourself, "Am I really happy, or do I 'think' I am happy?" Responses to such negative thoughts are likely to lead to self-fulfilling prophecies.

In such situations, you are likely to focus on small and minor differences between the two of us and blow them out of proportion in your mind. For example, your partner might like classical music, whereas you could be a rock music aficionado; that is a minor difference. And yet, your relationship anxiety could drive you to overemphasize this little point.

Reading too much into your words and actions - Overanalyzing and overthinking on what your partner says and does is an almost sure sign of relationship anxiety. For example, your partner may not be very fond of holding hands in public. But, if you read it as a sign of a lack of interest in you and your relationship, then it is possible you have anxiety issues.

Or, if both of you have decided to move in together and if your partner chooses to keep his or her old furniture, you could see it as a sign of your partner still holding on to his or her previous relationships. While these actions could be potential issues, overthinking them without ample evidence could be rooted in relationship anxiety.

Creating upheavals in your relationship - Deliberately creating upheavals or sabotaging your relationship could be rooted in anxiety. For example, you deliberately and needlessly pick arguments with your partner. Or you could push him or her away saying nothing is wrong even when you know you should discuss your problems with your partner.

You could test your partner toleration limits. For example, you could choose to meet up with your ex without informing your partner with no other underlying intention except to ruffle a few feathers. The reason why some of us indulge in such acts of sabotage is that we want to be reassured that our partner truly loves and cares for us.

Taking one of the above examples, you choose to push away your partner when he or she comes to comfort you because you want to know how much he or she will resist your efforts. Unfortunately, it is extremely difficult for anyone to pick up underlying motives such as these based on obvious acts of sabotage.

Missing out on enjoying the present state of the relationship - Another great way to check if you are buckling under the strain of relationship anxiety is to step back for a while. See if you are spending more time and energy worrying about the relationship than enjoying the current happy state. If the answer is yes, then it is time to take a relook at your attitude and find ways to take corrective action.

If you are unsure whether anxiety is playing a role in your attempts to create new or sustain old relationships, find answers to the following questions:

- Are you fazed by excessive worries that prevent you from seeking new relationships?

- Do you feel overwhelmingly anxious when your partner is away?

- Do you feel excessively anxious around sexual intimacy?

- Do you always depend on your partner to calm your anxiety or to reassure you that things are fine in the relationship?

- Are you continuously living in fear that your partner is going to leave or abandon you?

- Do you avoid talking about serious things with your partner because you are scared of conflict?

- Do you think hard and try and convince yourself that your partner is cheating on you even in the absence of any evidence?

If the answer to even one of the above questions is yes, then it is highly possible that you have relationship anxiety, which has the power to wreak havoc in your life, leaving you feeling lonely and sad. It is time to take up cudgels and fight off this menace and get the love you deserve in your life.

Causes of Relationship Anxiety

It is not easy at all to pinpoint any one particular cause of your relationship anxiety. Usually, multiple factors contribute to it. The only way you can get close enough to real causes is by investing time and energy on self-exploration and self-awareness.

And yet, as Astrid Robertson, a qualified, trained, and famed psychotherapist working in the realm of family and marriage therapy, puts it, "regardless of the cause or causes of relationship anxiety, the deepest underlying reason is an intense longing for connection and belonging."

However, it makes sense to look at some of the common causes of relationship anxiety. Read through them and see if you can relate to any of the listed items.

Previous relationship experiences - Many of us experience bad relationships and get over them too.

However, some of us might believe that we have overcome the painful effects of previous relationships, whereas, in reality, those agonizing experiences might still be nagging us at subconsciously driving us to become anxious with or in any relationship. If you have been hurt in a previous relationship, the memory of that pain is likely to trigger anxiety. Some of the common types of hurt that drive people into relationship anxiety include:

- Being cheated on by previous partners.

- Being misled about the nature of the relationship.

- Being lied to regarding their partner's true feelings.

- Being dumped unexpectedly and without any reason.

It is natural to find it difficult to trust another person if these painful memories continue to haunt us. This anxiety remains even if there is no real reason to believe that the current potential partner shows no inclination of doing anything to hurt us. Certain triggers in the brain continue to remind us of our past painful experiences, and we automatically begin to doubt and feel insecure.

This fear will prevent you from wanting to get into any long-term serious relationship. So, what if someone was to ask you this question, "How long does it take for two people to get into a serious relationship?" What if your answer is 'Never!" That could indicate you are going through the pangs of relationship anxiety driven by painful memories from the past that you simply cannot put out of your mind.

Clingy and needy - One of the most significant effects of relationship anxiety is that you become excessively clingy and needy towards your partner. The fear of losing your partner will drive you so crazy, you are scared to let him or her out of your sight even for a moment. You get scared that even a few minutes of silence can snowball into a breakup. The fear of abandonment makes us overly dependent on our partner. Some of the common examples of people with relationship anxiety tend to get worried about include:

- You get hyper if your partner does not reply to your messages instantly.

- You go out of the way to have dinner or lunch with your partner, sometimes, even to the extent of putting your job in jeopardy.

Understanding Relationship Anxiety

- Using the phrase 'I love you' frequently because you are scared that your partner will forget this truth and abandon you.

- Always wanting cuddles and hugs even in inappropriate places and situations.

- You demand to tag along with your partner when he or she is going to chill out with his or her friends.

- You get upset if your partner has to go on an outstation trip for official work.

One or more of the above cues demonstrate your clingy nature, which is driven by fear of abandonment.

Low self-esteem and self-confidence - If you are a person with low self-esteem, then too, you are likely to be bitten by the relationship anxiety bug. Research studies have shown that people with low self-esteem tend to doubt their partner's feelings, thanks to their self-doubting attitude. Referred to as projection in psychology, people with low self-esteem project their own lack of self-confidence onto their partners.

Typically, what this means is if you are disappointed and unhappy with the kind of person you are, it is easy to think that your partner feels the same about you. Interestingly, people with high self-esteem tend to use their relationship to affirm themselves. Which means to say, it is vital that you work on your self-esteem (which is spoken in some detail in another chapter in this book) to manage relationship anxiety.

Interestingly, anxiety and self-confidence are directly proportional to each other. The element of self-confidence can be a cause as well as an effect of anxiety. The lack of self-confidence increases relationship anxiety, and being constantly anxious, eats into self-confidence.

Attachment style - The attachment style you learned and experienced during your childhood significantly impacts your relationships as an adult. If your caregiver responded quickly to your needs as a child, it is likely that you developed a secure attachment style. Insecure attachment styles could contribute to relationship anxiety. It is important that you face and come to terms with any unresolved childhood problems that could be subconsciously causing relationship anxiety. Another chapter in this book deals exclusively with attachment styles and their effect on relationship anxiety.

Overly inquisitive, questioning attitude, and overanalyzing attitude - If you have a highly questioning or inquisitive nature, this too can contribute to relationship anxiety. For example, you could be a person who needs an answer to every question you have in mind before making a decision. Or, you need to consider all possible outcomes before choosing a path. This is a great thing because such an outlook helps you discern fact from fiction and make sensible choices.

Such an attitude helps you prepare yourself to handle all kinds of obstacles. However, if you begin to question everything, even after making your choice, then it is not a very healthy attitude to have. The problem starts when, despite having all the answers, you don't seem to be satisfied. An overthinking person is one who conjures up scenarios in his or her mind and takes actions on events and experiences that have not happened at all.

Getting stuck in an endless pattern of questions and answers will result in stagnation, and you will not be able to move ahead in your relationship. Anxiety is bound to set in sooner than later. Here is a classic example of a person with relationship anxiety on an overdose of questions and analysis. Suppose you are a girl of this kind.

You are on a first date with a guy who was introduced to you by a good friend and well-wisher who knows you really well. You dress well for the date, and so does this guy. You are as impressed with his conversation abilities and his wit as he is with yours. Then, the food arrives. As both of you tuck into your meal, your stream of questions start:

- Have you been in other relationships before this? If your date says yes, you look surprised.

- How many relationships have you been in?

- How did they end? Who called off the relationship first?

- Was there cheating involved?

More such innumerable questions will tumble from your mouth. And the primary reason to have the answers to these questions beforehand is that you are afraid of failing again. You want to glean as much information as you can about your potential partner so that you can see his personality with a fine-toothed comb and avoid any pitfalls that you may find. A perfect case of relationship anxiety manifesting itself!

And the worst thing is you have no control over your inquisitive nature. And that is the ultimate tragedy of the situation. You cannot control your negative thoughts from ruining your chances at love.

Effects of Anxiety on Relationships

If you are experiencing stress or strain in your relationship, it is likely that either you or her partner is having relationship anxiety. This anxiety can be a huge risk in your relationship. Here is how and why anxiety can ruin a relationship.

Anxiety breaks down trust between the partners - The fear and worry caused by anxiety results in your inability to connect with the true needs of the relationship at a given moment. Anxiety makes you less attuned to know and understand what you or your partner wants from the relationship.

If under the strain of anxiety, you feel overwhelmed, your partner is likely to see it as you being disinterested in him or her because you are not fully present or completely engaged with them at all times. In such circumstances, both of you tend to lose trust in each other, and that is the beginning of the end.

Anxiety suppresses your real thoughts and prevents you from articulating your true feelings. When you are anxious, you are bound to have trouble understanding your genuine thoughts and feelings as well as not being able to articulate your fears and concerns. You panic under the strain of excessive anxiety and find it very difficult to ask your partner for the space you need to get over your problems.

For example, suppose the discussion of a certain unpleasant event should ideally be put off for a while due to the present conditions not being conducive to the discussions. However, in your state of anxiety-driven fear and worry, you could end up insisting that the discussion right then and there, which, in turn, could result in disastrous and embarrassing scenarios both for you and your partner. Such experiences are common when either or both partners have relationship anxiety.

Moreover, since it is uncomfortable to manage anxiety, we tend to either not think about it or postpone it. However, the nagging effect remains in our minds, and every action and behavior of ours gets colored with the negative impacts of relationship anxiety. Also, not expressing your true feelings will only compound the negative emotions within you and could eventually spiral into something completely nasty and unpleasant.

Anxiety promotes selfishness - Anxiety is an excessive form of fear that is closely related to the fear of survival. Consequently, under the stress of such a powerful emotion, we tend to become very selfish, as we are too focused on our own needs that we cannot see or feel the needs of our partners. Your fears and worries put unnecessary pressure on you to protect yourself from potential pain and hurt, which, in turn, prevents you from showing compassion and kindness towards your partner and his or her needs.

In such circumstances, your partner is likely to mirror your behavior and attitude and would also become selfish because selfishness is one of the most contagious emotions. You can only imagine where this kind of relationship is headed!

Anxiety makes you angry and resentful - When you are anxious in love, one of the biggest side effects is anger and resentment. You end up hurting not only yourself but the person you care for the most in your life. Regardless of how much effort your partner makes to express his or her love for you, you always behave in ways that make him, or her feel terrible because you lose control over your anxiety-driven anger.

So, why are you always angry when you feel anxious? The answer is simple. Because under duress, your mind never gives you a break from dark and negative thoughts. Deep in your heart, you know that the anger you show is doing nothing but ruining the relationship more than ever. But you cannot stop yourself. Ironically, the fear of losing your loved one keeps your anger alive and kicking at all times, giving you no respite.

Anxiety makes you go that extra mile for your partner always - Love and romance are beautiful elements that can kindle joy and happiness between two people. After all, going the extra mile and preparing a surprise candle-lit or organizing a surprise birthday party for your partner is romantic and magical.

However, when anxiety drives you to go that extra mile for your partner, then it can be disastrous. Under the debilitating influence of anxiety, you are so caught up in trying to impress your partner, and to appear perfect in front of him or her, that you end up not only stressing yourself but also become someone who you are not.

You get so caught up in your anxiety to keep the relationship going that you forget to focus on the other aspects of your life, including friends, family, career, etc. You don't find the time or energy to pursue your interests and hobbies or even spend some quality time with your friends.

Not meeting with friends and family because of relationship anxiety could also be a result of your need to hide things from people. You are scared that when others see how desperate you are to stay in the relationship, they could try and show you the right path. In your present state of mind, that's not a path you want to tread.

The problem with such a behavior is that you don't focus on self-improvement at all, which could be counterproductive to your relationship. You are likely to come across as being immature and unprepared for a long-term, committed relationship, and the chances of your partner leaving you are high.

Anxiety takes away joy and happiness - Both of you are so caught up in the problems of the relationship (thanks to anxiety, fear, and worry) that you don't have the sense of unbridled freedom that is essential to feel joy and happiness. Anxiety limits us, and our feelings significantly so much so that the strain of bearing anxiety makes it very difficult to enjoy intimacy and sex. Not being able to engage fully with your partner also robs joy and happiness from your moments of togetherness.

Anxiety is the complete opposite of acceptance. Healthy levels of worry is a good thing for you because it grounds you as well as keeps you alert to elements that could help in improving the joy and happiness of your relationship. Worrying a little bit to keep your partner is good because it tells you that 'something is not right.'

This kind of healthy fear comes in the form of a tight knot in your stomach or a sharp pull in your heart (just the right amount). This pulling/tightening of the muscles in your body drives you to find out the root cause of any existing problem, along with probable solutions too.

Anxiety, on the other hand, makes you feel that a huge rock has found its place in your stomach and refuses to go away. You carry the burden of this emotional rock 24/7. This burden colors your perspective in such crazy ways that frequently you embrace things that could harm you and avoid things that could be good for you.

It is vital that you understand the effects of anxiety on your relationship so that you can take corrective measures and bring your relationship back on track. The good thing is that relationship anxiety can be overcome with a little bit of dedicated effort. This book is aimed at helping you understand the ways through which you can manage your relationship anxiety.

Also, it is important to remember that no relationship can be perfect and certain, and while this

Understanding Relationship Anxiety

fact seems a bit tough to accept, you must know that it is possible to silence the constant fear and chattering of your mind so that you can be calm. When you feel calm, and you have your emotions in check, the chances of making informed decisions that are good for you are high.

Chapter Two

Managing Relationship Anxiety - Acknowledgement, Negativity, and Jealousy

This story of mine is related to unwarranted panic attacks. Thanks to the previous relationship mishaps in my life, my anxiety levels were very high, and I was prone to panic attacks, many of whom were unwarranted and baseless. This story, however, led me to the person who helped me get over relationship anxiety. I am truly grateful to her.

But, my initial interactions with this friend of mine was not very good. I had met Sarah (I am going to call her that for ease of reference) at a family function, and we had hit off from the word go. She was funny, had loads of witty stories to share, and I realized I enjoyed being in her company.

I had already told her about my failed romances though I underplayed the anxiety I was experiencing. She said, "Hey, forget it! There are a lot more fish out there in the ocean. Let the old ones go." I remember laughing at this statement of hers. Of course, I knew she was joking and was only trying to help me see the fun part of my failures.

Then, out of the blue, she told me that she knows this great guy who is also looking out for a good partner. She asked me, "Would you like to check him out? I could easily set up a blind date with him." I hesitated for a while. But soon, her vivacity infected me, and I decided to take up the challenge. I told myself, "What is the worst thing that can happen on this blind date? Perhaps, there wouldn't be a second date, that's all." I convinced myself in this way and decided to go and check out this guy Sarah was setting up for me.

Armed with all the confidence I could muster, I turned up nicely dressed for the date, or so I thought. I arrived on time at the designated pub-cum-diner. It was a nice place, although a bit noisy for a first date. My doubt was how can we talk in the noise. How can I get all the answers to the questions I had in mind for him?

Anyway, I thought I would find a way once he comes. Ignoring my palpitating heart, I ordered a coke and took a seat at the bar, waiting for my date to turn up. After waiting for 10 minutes, I started to panic because my date hadn't yet turned up. Was he going to ditch me on the first date itself? Why didn't he turn up? Did Sarah get the place wrong? No, she was smart and wouldn't make such silly mistakes, I thought. There must be another reason for this.

My anxiety was created a lot of self-doubts. I was wondering if my dress was fine. Was I looking too fat or too thin? Did I have on too much makeup? Was I looking like a vamp? A million questions bombarded my brain. Still, I waited for 30 more minutes trying to calm down my anxiety and murmurings of panic that had started to creep into my mind.

And then, out of the blue, I had this horrifying thought that threatened to throttle my self-confidence and self-esteem. My inner critic voice (you will learn more about this in another chapter of this book) began to prod me mercilessly. I started thinking that maybe this supposed date might have peeked through the window, saw me, and decided that I was too ugly to waste his time to get to know me. Anyway, it was a no from his side. So why waste time and money on me?

He might have decided to just move on even without meeting with me. Was I so ugly and horrible that people didn't even want to have a date with me once? I felt suffocated and couldn't breathe because of all these debilitating negative thoughts.

Managing Relationship Anxiety - Acknowledgement, Negativity, and Jealousy

I looked at everyone at the bar and thought they were mocking me. Their looks seemed to say, "What kind of loser would sit at a bar alone with a coke? And look at her; she is still waiting with that coke, hoping another loser will come forward to date her." With all these thoughts threatening to suffocate me, I reached the pinnacle of my panic attack. In that panic state, I rushed out of the place, managed to get a cab somehow through my tears, went home, got under the sheet, and wept myself to sleep.

The residual pangs of fear and anxiety remained in my head, along with a splitting headache when I woke up the next morning. I called in sick and decided to stay in and mop in my own sad company. I looked at my phone and realized that Sarah had been trying to call me the entire night. There were 24 missed calls.

I did not call her back because I didn't want to talk about being stood up because my date peeked through the window and didn't like my ugly face. Yes, I had decided and was sure that was the only reason my date didn't turn up. I was sure she wanted me to tell her everything, and I couldn't bring myself to confess that I know that he saw me through the window and ran off.

Poor Sarah! She even came home and rang the bell a couple of times. I simply pretended I was not at home and did not open the door.

But I couldn't keep running away from my dear, dear friend and well-wisher because she wouldn't give up on me. She cared and loved me enough to be patient and wait for the pain I felt to subside and then drive sense into me. One day, she accosted me on the street, and I had no option but to confess my fears and anxieties to her.

Sarah allayed my fears and then made me laugh at my own imagination. She told me, "Hello, my tribal friend! Which forest does your tribe come from? Do you even realize that we are living in the 21st century with advanced technology at our fingertips? We are not living in the Medieval Ages, where the only way you can get information secretly is by peeking through windows."

"If your date wanted to see you before walking into the pub, he needn't have peeked through the window. All he had to do was look up your profile on any of the social media platforms! You forgot you have a profile on Facebook, Instagram, and others. One glance at your profile would have told him what he wanted to know. And then he could've used any sensible excuse

Managing Relationship Anxiety - Acknowledgement, Negativity, and Jealousy

not to turn up instead of coming all the way and then peeking through the window!"

It was then that I realized how deeply affected I was by my unwarranted panic attacks. I just couldn't think straight and formed irrational and baseless conclusions. Then Sarah also told me that the reason my date couldn't turn up was that he met with an accident. She tried to call me so many times that night to tell me and here I was giving in to my unwarranted panic attacks thoughtlessly.

Therefore, one of the first things you must do to overcome relationship anxiety is to understand what anxiety is.

Take Note of and Acknowledge Your Anxiety

What is Anxiety? At a very basic level, anxiety is nothing but an evolutionary self-protective response to danger. Human beings have survived through millennia, thanks to the power that anxiety renders us with. Yes, anxiety is powerful if understood rightly and balanced well.

Anxiety promotes the fight-flight response by preparing our body and mind to run from or protect ourselves in the face of imminent danger. It engages all our physical and mental energy resources so that we can run or stay and fight, depending on the danger that we are faced with.

So, it is easy to understand why anxiety is not a very good place to be in and why none of us like it. It is, after all, a cue for your body to prepare itself for a dangerous and unpleasant experience. Who wants to deal with such cues, right? Now, even though we have evolved far enough to handle and overcome most of the dangers that our ancestors faced, our bodily responses haven't changed much.

So, even if the dangers have altered their shape, your biological response is more or less the same as those of your ancestors. The next time you feel anxious, pay attention to your body and notice all the changes that take place. Invariably, the changes would include many of the following:

- Clenched of your jaws
- Shoulder muscles tensing up
- Tightening of the throat
- Fast and shallow breathing
- Sweaty palms

The next time you feel anxious, focus on your physical symptoms. You cannot really prevent the physical changes from happening. But, being aware of the bodily changes can give you a clue that you are getting anxious, and you need to be on your guard when it comes to negative thoughts and powerful emotions overwhelming you.

By taking note of your physical symptoms, you can take the necessary steps to prevent a mild anxiety attack from becoming a full-blown, uncontrollable one.

The next step is to focus on your emotions. When you feel anxious, what are the emotions playing in your mind? The emotions are likely to cover a range, including anger, sadness, fear, insecurity, distress, frustration, fatigue, numbness, jealousy, shame, embarrassment, and more.

Use this list to narrow down the emotion playing predominantly in your mind to the best extent possible. If the emotion doesn't fit into anyone mentioned in this list, prepare a bigger list of feelings and keep them ready so that you can use it to try and identify the predominant emotion you feel at the time of the set-in of anxiety.

After you have identified and labeled it, sit with the emotion for a while. Most often, the emotions you feel are a complex combination of many feelings. Try and break down the whole complex and identify each of the emotions. Don't forget to write it down. This activity of identifying and labeling your emotions will help you connect with them as well as prevent you from falling into the dark abyss that they are capable of hurling you into from which it is difficult to come out.

Next, try and identify the triggers that brought on the physical and emotional responses to anxiety. Write down what happened that set off the trigger of anxiety. Look at the situation as objectively as possible. Imagine that you are explaining the situation to your best friend. What would you say to him or her?

It is important to remove the emotions connected with the situation. Make sure what you write is not your opinion but the exact event that happened. A great way to do this is to pretend you are a robot with no feelings. How would this robotic machine write down the event?

What exactly was it that happened that made you feel what you felt? What are the assumptions you made that lacked were not fact- or evidence-based? Let us look at a simple example of such an event.

Managing Relationship Anxiety - Acknowledgement, Negativity, and Jealousy

Suppose you sent your partner a text message that he or she hasn't yet replied to. Your body started reacting, showing symptoms of anxiety, as explained above. Emotions of fear and insecurity began to play on your mind. You have also pinpointed the event precisely as being the non-responsiveness from your partner to your message.

Remember, the trigger of anxiety is only your partner not responding to your message. Your assumptions like, "My partner has not texted me because he or she doesn't love me." Or "My partner wants to teach me a lesson of what it is to feel abandoned or left" have contributed to your anxiety attack.

So, the next step to do is to examine the evidence behind your assumptions. For example, the reason behind the assumptions is that your partner has behaved like this in the past. He or she has chosen not to reply to your messages just to spite you. So, your assumptions could be vindicated. You need to continue your investigation on the matter.

Alternately, ask yourself if these assumptions are based merely on your experiences from your previous relationships. Ask yourself if these assumptions are rooted in your own anxieties. Are your thoughts going something like this?

- My partner is not texting me because he or she thinks I am not good enough to have a relationship with them.

- In fact, I know I am not good enough for any relationship.

- My partner has found someone else because I am not good enough, and that is why he is not responding to my message.

These assumptions are sure to trigger relationship anxiety that has no basis, at least not at that point in time.

On the other hand, you know that your partner does not check his or her phone often in the office, and therefore, that is the most probable reason for not getting a response to your message. The anxious feeling is automatically lifted.

If you notice, the primary reason for doing this exercise is to identify, acknowledge, and engage with all the elements of relationship anxiety. Now, you take these pieces of evidence and your thoughts and emotions and re-evaluate them to see if the origin of my anxiety is accurate or not. The more you do this, the more you learn about yourself, and the more you are able to manage your anxiety. By doing this, you pay attention to and acknowledge that you have a problem and that you need to work on it and overcome it at the earliest.

Managing Negative Thoughts

So, you have managed to re-evaluate your evidence and thoughts. Your logical mind is telling you that your thoughts and emotions are not really evidence-based. And yet, you find it difficult to believe your logical mind, which is totally relatable and understandable. Emotions, after all, are powerful and can easily convert your logical mind to think otherwise.

Moreover, your feelings and thoughts are yours, and therefore, true in your life. You have to manage your negative thoughts and realign them in ways that will help you overcome relationship anxiety and not be overwhelmed by it. So, let us move on and see how you can manage negative thoughts.

Identify and Recognize Thought Distortions

The human mind is not just clever but persistent when it comes to convincing us that thoughts are real and true, even in the absence of evidence and facts. These inaccurate thoughts empower negative emotions and negative thinking. So it is imperative that you identify and recognize these thought distortions:

Perceiving everything as being black and white - Seeing everything in black and white means invariably translates to a lack of tolerance. Do you see everything as being completely good or completely bad? Do you view people as either totally lovable or hate-worthy? Such thought distortions can be dangerous for you. You need to include black, white, and everything in-between as well to really know, understand, and love your world and the people in it. Examples of such thoughts would be like:

- Gone case! There is nothing we can do to help here (there is always something we can do to help in some little way).

- This will always work (remind yourself nothing works forever).

- That man is pure evil (no one is pure evil or pure good; we are all an imperfect combination)

Filtering - People who filter their thoughts are those who focus only on the negative aspects of situations. People who use mental filtering tend to discount the positive aspects of any given situation. Often, they use the concept of luck or fluke to explain clearly obvious and unmistakable positive outcomes.

Using 'should' statements - Observe your thoughts closely and see how often the word 'should' or 'ought' come into your mind. These words usually make you believe that you didn't or say enough. Examples of such 'should' or 'ought' thoughts include:

- I should have done that too.
- I ought to have pitched in.
- I should have stopped her or him.

If you notice, these kinds of thoughts have a self-chastising quality about them. It takes a negative view of situations.

Personalizing everything - For example, if someone did not smile back at you, then if you could think that you have done something to upset him or her. This is the meaning of personalizing and taking things personally. If you take everything around you personally, you are likely to blame yourself for all that is happening around you. It is not a nice situation to be in. Examples of such thoughts:

- It is all my fault.

- He or she hates me because I am not good enough.

- The world hates me.

- I am responsible for this.

Catastrophizing - People who catastrophize assume the worst thing about any given situation. When you catastrophize, even simple, ordinary anxieties get to you. For example, if your partner has not replied to one text message, then immediately, your thoughts may go like this, "Oh God! I am sure he is going to leave me! That is why he is not responding to my message."

Mind-reading - Sometimes, especially if communication in your relationship is not good, mind-reading becomes the norm for both partners. You tend to misread or misinterpret nonverbal cues (even when there is no conversation going on). For example, if your partner has a frown on her face as she is watering her plants, you think that she is angry at you for something. This thought drives up anxiety levels unnecessarily.

Emotional reasoning - Some of us have the tendency to look at everything around us through the

Managing Relationship Anxiety - Acknowledgement, Negativity, and Jealousy

lens of our emotions and feelings. For example, if you are sad about something, you look at everything around you with the same sadness. The reverse is also true. If you are excessively happy about something, you could see everything in a positive light, even those that should not be seen this way.

It is vital that you keep out emotions as much as possible, especially when you are discussing something really important or are in the process of decision-making. Interestingly, emotional reasoning is commonly used by nearly all of us, including those who don't have a relationship anxiety issue.

Look at these thought distortions and see if your thinking process fits into one or more of them. Be aware of thoughts so that you can manage them and make suitable alterations in your thinking process so that you don't get caught up in the mire of your negative thoughts.

Stay with the Negative Thought for a While

One of the most effective ways of handling negative thoughts is to stay with it for a while. While you do this, remember not to react or respond to the thought. Just look at the thought and watch it grow in size in your mind.

When it reaches a peak, either it will disappear immediately or slowly lose its power and go away gradually from your mind. Then, take your mind off this thought and continue with your work. It is likely that this thought enters your mind again. Repeat the above exercise with it. Soon, you will become friends with this thought, and it will cease to disturb you!

Challenge Negative Thoughts

Each time you get hit by a negative thought, stop and evaluate it for accuracy. If your best friend came to you with this negative thought, what kind of rebuttals would you offer him or her? Imagine you are dealing with your best friend and give yourself the same rebuttals.

Are you assuming worst-case scenarios and taking on a catastrophic view on things? Are you taking things personally and feeling hurt? Are you blaming yourself for the wrong things happening in your relationship? Now, turn around and think of the positive things that have taken place. These positive thoughts challenge your negative thoughts, bringing a semblance of balance in your thinking process.

Avoid Judgments

Human beings have evolved to stand in judgment of everything and everyone around them. We cannot resist judging ourselves and the people around us. We constantly compare ourselves and use these comparisons to feel superior or inferior to others, depending on the situation. Such an attitude is bound to breed unhappiness and dissatisfaction, and both these elements creep into every other aspect of your life, especially your relationships.

So, when you come across a judgmental thought, look at it, and let it go without agreeing or disagreeing with it. Another way to stop yourself from judging yourself or other people is to counter every negative thought you have with a positive one. For example, if your thought about yourself goes something like, "I am no good," counter it with at least one good thing you know for sure you possess. Balancing positive and negative judgments can also help to create a balanced outlook.

Focus on your Strengths and Plus-Points

We human beings are made to dwell on the negative aspects of everything and overlook the positive aspects. You have to make an effort to reverse this trend of thinking consciously. Focus on your positives and strengths. What are you good at? Why do some people like you a lot?

Find answers to such questions and focus on your good qualities. The more you do this, the more confidence you will build, and the easier it will get to love yourself. You will feel more positive about yourself than before, which, in turn, will compel you to take control of your life and make it go in the direction you want it to. Also, you will cease to wallow in self-pity, an element that is part and parcel of relationship anxiety.

Practice Gratitude

Being and demonstrating an attitude of gratitude is a proven method to counter negative thoughts. Every time you face a challenge in your life, shift your focus on things that you should be grateful for. These things need not be something profound or great. It could be anything small, including:

- The opportunity to live another day

- The love of your family and loved ones

- The job that keeps you afloat

- The lovely music you can hear that many others in the world do not have access to

- The wonderful weather outside

Managing Relationship Anxiety - Acknowledgement, Negativity, and Jealousy

- Access to basic amenities like good food and clean water that many others do not have

I agree that some of these thoughts are too broad to get them during emotionally challenging times. You tend to overlook these small things. That is precisely why you must shift your thoughts from your debilitating negative emotions and focus on a multiple of other positive things that you should be grateful for. When you do this, your problems will automatically reduce in size, and the negativity will be released from your system.

Negative thoughts can affect you only to the extent you allow them to. You are the way out of your negative thoughts, and they cannot control you unless you let them. Countering your negative thoughts might seem like an arduous task initially. But, with persistent practice and dedicated efforts, you will see that this activity is not difficult at all.

Managing Jealousy in a Relationship

Jealousy is not always a bad thing because it has the power to work hard to achieve what the person you are jealous of has. It is also a natural emotion, especially so in romantic relationships, and even more so when you are under the strain of relationship anxiety.

Jealousy is not restricted in romantic relationships to fears about your partner liking someone else other than you. It also includes the feelings of jealousy you have towards your partner because you believe he or she is having a better life, a better job, and better success than you.

Thanks to social media platforms, jealousy can take on a hideous face driven by the amount of publicity that people tend to get for themselves on these platforms. These platforms increase the complexity of romantic relationships more than ever, even as they enhance your relationship anxiety. Let us see how you can learn to curb jealousy and prevent it from ruining a perfectly good existing or potential relationship.

Recognize and Assess your Jealousy

When we label jealousy, it loses its power. When we identify and acknowledge it, we take the first step to eliminate it from our life and relationship.

Next, assess your jealousy. Why are you jealous of someone? Is it because they have a gift or talent that you want? If yes, then do something about it and work hard to get what you want. For example, if your partner praises another person for playing the guitar well, do you feel a pang of jealousy? Why? Because you want to play the guitar too, or do you want to get praised by your partner?

If you want to play the guitar, join a class. If you want to be praised by the partner just like he or she praised the other person, find out what you can do to earn it and work towards it. When you assess your jealousy and find out the reason for it, you can then take action to achieve your desire. The root of the jealousy is taken out when you do this.

Let Go of Jealousy

Sometimes, the best way to get rid of this emotion is to let go of it. Remind yourself that you have enough problems on your plate and don't need jealousy to be added to it. Breathe deeply, imagine the feeling of jealousy leaving your system, and watch it as it goes further away from your life.

Each time you are affected by jealously, breathe deeply, and repeat the exercise, and let it go out of your life. Do this until jealously truly and really leaves you for good.

Remind Yourself of your Own Strengths

Maybe you cannot learn to play the guitar as well as the other person did. It doesn't matter. There are many other things you can do. Remind yourself of your own strengths. Be proud of and embrace yourself the way you are. You are unique and special, and no one can be YOU.

Remember that jealousy is a very common trait found in all human beings. The trick is in not being overwhelmed by it. Recognize it and do what you need to do before it takes control of your life and your relationships.

Chapter Three

Managing Relationship Anxiety - Healthy Boundaries, Couple Conflicts, and Insecurity

When talking about setting clear boundaries, one particularly bad experience comes to mind. This experience taught me many things about setting powerful, healthy limits that enhance my self-confidence and self-esteem, including how not to act stupidly just to hit back at someone.

Multiple failed relationships hardly helped me manage my anxieties. I kept falling off the wagon as it were and continued to fall for the wrong men, hurting myself repeatedly, and not being able to learn lessons well. Thanks to Sarah, I was able to at least share my pain with one person.

She always made me see the funny side of things, and we would laugh together for a while. Then, she would inspire me to look at the experience objectively and see what lessons I can learn from it so that I can avoid or be prepared to handle a similar situation in the future. Now back to this story, that taught me crucial lessons on building boundaries.

I was in a relationship with a man (I am going to call him Kevin), who loved his friends a lot. In fact, there were times when I believed that he loved his friends more than anyone else in the world except for himself! Anyway, this specific partner would go out every Saturday with his friends and return way past midnight.

So many times, I would have wanted to go out for a movie with him or just to have a quiet Saturday dinner at home. But I never got a single Saturday night with him. Aah yes! I did get one Saturday night with that boyfriend. He had an attack of food poisoning and was puking continuously.

Obviously, he couldn't go out that night and was forced to stay in with me. Well, it was stupid of me to have expected any fireworks that night. But I did! And the only fireworks I got were the horrible, gagging noises he made as he visited the loo a zillion times to empty his stomach. That was the night I wished he had actually gone out instead of retching his way into my heart and mind.

Other than that Saturday, Kevin was out every Saturday. He didn't bother to check with me if I had any plans. And I also didn't offer to accompany him. Well, not that I didn't want to. I was dying to go out every Saturday night. Who would want to stay in and watch some boring old rerun on television when great Saturday nights with friends and loved ones are beckoning you?

But I was too scared to ask anything for myself because I didn't want to appear jealous or clingy, which might give him a reason to end the relationship. I just pretended that I didn't care but continued to feel the pain and agony of loneliness every time he went out with his friends without even a word of apology or explanation. In fact, I can never forget one specific Saturday when I tried to know about his night plans through a roundabout way.

"Darling, what would you like for dinner today," I started on Saturday morning.

"Make anything you like," he replied nonchalantly.

"Would you like a pot roast and some bread pudding for dessert?" I asked.

"Yeah! Ok, sounds good!"

His reply cheered me up no end. I took that as an indication that he would stay with me at home instead of going out with his friends. So, I went into the trouble of cooking pot roast. The tantalizing smell from the kitchen was unmissable. I could have sworn that I saw Kevin sniff many times as the smell pervaded the little apartment. The roast came out perfect, and so did the bread pudding. I even ordered a little bit of ice-cream to go with the pudding.

I laid out the table at around 8 and was just about to call out to Kevin when he came out of the bedroom, fully dressed to go out as usual. He didn't even glance at the table.

"What about dinner?" I asked meekly.

"Oh! You eat and leave my share in the microwave. I will eat when I return." Saying this, he walked out of the house without batting an eyelid.

The tears stung so bad that I thought my heart would break!

But, the idiot that I was, I didn't say a word and did exactly what he told me to. Of course, I couldn't eat any food. I just left some food for him in the microwave. Then, I crept under the bedsheet and cried myself to sleep.

One day, a colleague of mine organized an outing for some of us from the workplace. When Kevin heard of this office outing, I was planning on going, he flipped. He got so angry that he started accusing all the men in my office as being flirts. He said that all these men organize these kinds of get-togethers only to flirt with the women. After hurling a string of abuses on my colleagues, Kevin forbade me to go warning me that these parties would be nothing more than a place where men will pounce and assault ready women.

Something snapped inside me that day. For a change, I didn't meekly agree to his demands. But I recalled all those Saturday nights I spend alone at home while he had a gala time with his friends. Miraculously, I stood my ground and decided to go despite his obvious seething fury.

And I went only to realize that this party was the exact opposite of what Kevin had warned me. The men were fine while the women of my office came dressed to kill, sorry not kill, but murder. They came dressed like prostitutes from the seedy clubs of Caracas wearing such tight-fitting clothes that I thought they would have a hard time breathing!

I was definitely bored at the party for a reason very different from what Kevin told me. But bored all the same as I watched simple office folk suddenly (and quite sadly too) transforming themselves into horny cat women hoping frantically they will catch their batman that day.

So, you see, I realized the importance of drawing clear boundaries in a relationship so that I don't get taken for granted. I also learned the importance of not doing something based on emotion just to hit back at someone, which is also part of setting healthy boundaries that respect each partner's space and freedom.

Managing relationship anxiety requires a multi-pronged approach. The chapter two dealt with understanding anxiety and its effects on your body and mind, how to manage negative thoughts and jealousy. Here, we will look at three more elements, namely setting healthy boundaries, managing couple conflicts, and managing insecurity.

Setting Healthy Boundaries

Relationship anxiety plays a big role in setting clear, healthy boundaries. Partners with relationship anxiety tend to underplay their needs because of fears of abandonment. They tend to keep their needs under wraps with some not even acknowledging their own needs in the hope of keeping their partners happy so that he or she doesn't get a 'reason' to leave them.

Managing Relationship Anxiety - Healthy Boundaries, Couple Conflicts, and Insecurity

One of the most common misconceptions in romantic relationships is the misplaced belief that personal boundaries are redundant elements. In fact, most of us believe that personal boundaries are counterproductive to healthy relationships. This belief is a total myth, and we will see the importance of personal boundaries and how they help in building strong, meaningful, long-term romantic relationships.

Personal boundaries, according to psychologists, let you know the space that you are responsible for and the spaces that you or both of you are accountable for. Without this line, there is bound to be confusion in the relationship. The lack of these boundaries leaves partners confused about the responsibilities and accountabilities of each of them.

It is important to note that these boundaries are not walls or fences. They are clearly set and understood by both partners. The boundaries are also respected. In fact, the partners are allowed to cross over the boundaries in times of need based on mutual understanding. However, when these boundaries are crossed over to take advantage of or to harm the other person, then the problems in relationships begin.

In relationships, boundaries are set for the following reasons:

- They help partners to seek permission before crossing the boundaries set by their partners, which, in turn, builds mutual respect and trust.

- Boundaries demonstrate the respect and importance given to each other's feelings, differences of opinions, and perspectives.

- Boundaries help partners show their gratitude for each other.

A relationship without boundaries results in partners taking each other for granted. Each partner assumes that his or her partner thinks and works in the same way as he or she does. Partners don't realize that by frequently and mindlessly crossing boundaries, they are violating healthy relationship codes.

Boundaries in romantic relationships are more important than in other relationships because people live and inhabit each other's most intimate sexual, physical, and emotional spaces. It is, therefore, vital that boundaries in relationships get clearly defined and accepted by both partners.

Managing Relationship Anxiety - Healthy Boundaries, Couple Conflicts, and Insecurity

While setting boundaries, it is crucial to know that certain kinds don't really work in relationships. Some examples are explained as follows:

- Boundaries that use 'always, never, forever' are unrealistic and will not pass the test of time. For example, if you tell your partner that he or she can 'never' come late from his or her workplace, it will obviously not work.

- Boundaries that demonstrate double standards are not allowed too. For example, coming late from the workplace is alright for male partners, and not alright for female partners will never work.

- Also, boundaries that are used to manipulate each other will not work. For example, if you tell your partner that if he or she comes home from work after 7, then you will not have sex.

- Ambiguous and vaguely-worded boundaries also don't work. For example, telling your partners something like, "You have to do household chores at least a few times every week," is vague. Boundaries have to be made specific like, "Washing dishes is your responsibility, and doing laundry is mine."

When boundaries are not set, we assume that partners know everything we want. For example, if you want your accomplishments to be recognized, then you must tell your partner this in clear terms. Instead of telling him or her, if you simply mope around when this need of yours is not fulfilled, there is bound to be anxiety in the relationship.

How to set clear and healthy boundaries in a relationship? Here are some useful tips for you.

Build self-awareness - One of the first steps you need to take before you can create healthy boundaries is to know yourself. What are your likes and dislikes? What are you comfortable with, and what conditions and behaviors make you uncomfortable? What are your needs and desires? What scares you? How would you want to be treated as an individual, as a partner?

Communicate your needs clearly - Once you are clear about your needs, then ensure you articulate them without any ambiguity to your existing or potential partner too. Most often, violations of boundaries are rooted in unclear expectations and misunderstandings, both of which can be overcome by open, honest communication.

At this juncture, it makes sense to remind yourself that not setting healthy boundaries through honest communication is actually counterproductive to overcoming relationship anxiety. So, don't hesitate to tell your partners about your needs and desires.

Also, be specific about your needs. Here are some examples of how you can use clear, specific language to set healthy boundaries:

- Please don't read my personal diary. I feel my privacy is violated when you do so.

- I love you. However, I cannot call in sick at my workplace to stay with you while you overcome your hangover.

- If you put your clothes in the laundry basket by Saturday noon every week, I will happily take them down to the laundromat for you.

- I am busy with something right now. Just give me 15 minutes, and then I can give you my full attention, and you can tell me about your day at the office.

Don't hesitate to tell your partner that you love him or her. However, you care a lot about your boundaries as well. For example, if your girlfriend flared up at you when she saw you meet your ex, you can say something like, "I can talk to you about this incident provided you handle your anger. I don't like it when you get angry and attack me without speaking to me about what is bothering you."

Use 'I' statements instead of 'you' statements. For example, say, "I would appreciate it if you didn't throw your wet towel on the bed," instead of saying, "You are always throwing your wet towel on the bed." Instead of saying, "You need to....," try and say, "I would really like it if you can...."

Of course, these methods of talking need not always work. However, they are likely to garner a more receptive response than using criticism. Open communication towards setting healthy boundaries fosters happy, contented relationships in which anxiety will have little or no part to play.

Managing Couple Conflicts

Disagreements, fights, and conflicts are part and parcel of any romantic relationship, and trying to avoid them is like trying to live without breathing. It is impossible to avoid conflicts. In fact, avoiding them could be work against your dream to be in a fulfilling, meaningful, long-term relationship.

Yes, conflicts have a lot of good in them, which can be harnessed to build a fabulous relationship. On the contrary, avoiding conflicts will only serve to build

Managing Relationship Anxiety - Healthy Boundaries, Couple Conflicts, and Insecurity

anxiety in a relationship. Of course, conflicts should not rule your relationship. They need to be managed.

Before we go on to seeing how we can manage conflicts, let us see the good side of health conflicts that have the power to bring intimacy and increased love in your relationship. Here are some ways that healthy conflicts can contribute productively to your relationship.

- It increases trust between couples. Constructive conflicts based on respecting personal boundaries ensure both partners get the opportunity to express their needs, views, and opinions on elements affecting the relationship.

- Knowing that both of you can argue over something without the underlying love and trust being disturbed is a sign of the depth of your relationship. Such an attitude ensures conflicts remain healthy and don't get ugly.

- Both of you will feel better after a conflict. It releases anxiety, tension, and fear after both partners speak out their minds and the things that worried each of them. Many couples feel like a weight has been lifted off from their shoulders after they have had an argument.

- Conflicts increase intimacy in the relationship. When both of you know each other's deepest thoughts and reasons for worry and anxiety, it is likely that both of you will work towards reducing the fears. Consequently, understanding and intimacy between the partners will increase.

- Conflicts can improve the characters of both partners. When you use conflicts as a personality growth element, then both of you are learning from each other. You realize the things you are doing wrong, and your partner also gets to know about himself or herself.

And yet, managing conflict in relationships is an essential component of harnessing the advantages mentioned above. So, how can you manage conflicts between couples? Here are some pointers to help you.

Talk about your feelings without blaming your partner - For example, if your partner's frequent late-coming is making you anxious, the ideal way to express this would be, "I feel anxious and worried when you come home late from work. It hurts me when you don't share your worries with me."

If you are jealous of your girlfriend spending time with her boss instead of with you, telling her, "You are behaving irrationally," is putting her in a defensive mode, which will lead to a competitive attitude. Instead, if you said, "I feel jealous when you spend more time with your boss," you are not only being honest about your feelings for your girlfriend but also are not impugning her character.

The conversation after such a statement is likely to take place constructively as both of you sit down and sort out issues in the relationship.

Do not use generic words like 'always,' 'never,' etc. - Examples of such statements that should be avoided are:

- You are always doing this to me.

- You are never on time.

- You are always looking at your mobile phone.

- You never help me in the kitchen.

- You spend all weekends with your friends.

These statements do not prompt a healthy discussion. They only lead to both partners taking offensive/defensive stances with each other leading to painful and avoidable conflicts.

Choose one issue at a time - Constructive conflicts can happen only one issue at a time. If you combine and mix multiple issues together, then there is likely to a mess you will find difficult to clean up. It is not easy to do this because it is natural for the conversation to flow from one topic to another, especially in the heat of the moment. However, you must be conscious about it and stick it one issue during discussions with your partner.

Listen to your partner - Listening skills form an essential element of a happy, healthy relationship. When you listen to your partner, pay full attention to him or her. Listen to the verbal and the nonverbal cues your partner is sending your way. Paraphrase what he or she is saying to ensure there is no misunderstanding or misinterpretation.

You can also learn to interpret your partner's reactions and repeat it for the benefit of both of you. For example, if you notice your boyfriend is frowning at a comment of yours, then you can say something like, "You are angry at my comment, right?" Listening to each other is a sign of a healthy understanding and respect for each other's opinions and ideas, and this will go a long way in reducing anxiety and create a fulfilling relationship.

Managing Relationship Anxiety - Healthy Boundaries, Couple Conflicts, and Insecurity

Look at things from their perspective - Not only should you make an effort to practice active listening, especially when you are in a conflict state with your partner, you must also try and see things from his or her perspective. Look at the situations as objectively as possible, minus your emotions and see how they seem. You will notice a difference in the way things appear when you look at them objectively.

In fact, multiple studies have been conducted with married couples wherein they were asked to write down their impressions of a situation in their marriage as it would be seen by a third party. Couples who were able to view situations in this manner were more likely to have a long-term, sustained relationship compared to those who could not write down a situation objectively.

Avoid interrupting your partner's speech - When your partner is telling you something, let him or her finish saying it entirely before putting forth your ideas and counter-arguments. While it is difficult to not to get defensive, especially when we are criticized, you must remind yourself that a defensive attitude solves nothing.

Letting your partner complete what he or she started to say will help in releasing pent-up stress and anxiety. After this, it is likely that your partner will realize the frivolity of his or her complaints. Many times, arguments are just a way of venting out frustrations. Therefore, don't stop this venting out process in the middle because it will only make matters worse.

Conflicts are healthy aspects of any relationship, and the key to keeping healthy and civil is to manage them prudently. Two critical elements needed for effective conflict management in a relationship are anger management and looking at things from all perspectives. However, eliminating conflicts entirely could lead to accumulated stress and anxiety. Use conflicts to air out each other's frustrations even as you respect one another's boundaries.

Managing Insecurity

Insecurity is a sense of inadequacy you feel about yourself. We feel threatened because of this insecurity we have about ourselves. Self-doubt is a common emotion all of us feel at some time or the other in our lives. However, feeling insecure without rhyme or reason and chronically can turn your life into hell. Moreover, it will negatively impact your relationships, especially romantic ones.

Managing Relationship Anxiety - Healthy Boundaries, Couple Conflicts, and Insecurity

Insecurity takes away peace and happiness from your relationship, and you find it exceedingly difficult to engage completely with your partner meaningfully. You find it difficult to relax in front of your partner. Feeling insecure leads to jealousy too. You end up accusing and blaming your partner for everything, and you always need reassurance from him or her that things are going fine. Insecurity erodes trust and is really, really bad for a relationship.

So, how can you overcome this debilitating feeling of insecurity? Here are some easy tips to follow.

Take stock of your strengths - When we feel insecure, our focus is mostly on our weaknesses and the things we lack. You must remind yourself that all great relationships are those wherein each partner brings in his or her own set of skills and strengths that add value to the partnership. Each partner's skills invariably complement those of the other partner.

Partners in a great relationship are equal to each other but in different ways. The sum total of all strengths of the two partners is what builds the relationship and makes or breaks it.

So, to get rid of your insecure feeling in a relationship, the first thing to do is take stock of the value you bring to it. Don't worry too much about beauty, wealth, and other materialistic things you may or may not have. Those can be bought or earned easily in today's highly resourceful markets. What you need to focus on is the power and strength of character you possess that makes the relationship meaningful and fulfilling to your partner.

List down the character traits you possess that enhances the joy and happiness of the relationship. Are you fun to be with? Are you kind and generous? Are you compassionate? Are you a great communicator? Do you make your partner feel loved and wanted? These are the elements that people look for and value in a wholesome relationship.

Focus on the things you have and take your mind off of the things you lack. This approach will shift your perspective, and you are likely to feel less insecure than before. And also remember if your partner does not value your contribution, then that is his or her problem; in fact, it is your partner's loss. You find solace in the strength of your own power and self-value.

Don't give up your independence - A healthy relationship has two healthy people in it. Getting involved in your relationship without regard to your own needs and boundaries is bound to result in a diffused sense of your personality, which is an important contributor to insecurity. Maintain your independence with regard to who you are and what you do. When you know that you are not dependent on the relationship for all your needs, the sense of insecurity will fade.

Maintaining your independence means you have things other than the relationship going on in your life. This approach not only builds your sense of well-being but also makes you an interesting and attractive partner to have a relationship with. Your sense of independence could come in a variety of ways, including:

• Making time for your own set of friends

• Having your own interests and hobbies

• Being financially independent

• Self-improvement goals which are different from relationship-improvement goals

The trick is to be yourself first. Only then can you add value to someone else.

Trust yourself - Feeling safe and secure in a relationship is mostly about trusting your partner.

However, it is equally important that you trust yourself. You must learn to trust yourself so deeply that you believe that, regardless of what happens with the relationship, you can take care of yourself.

Trust your instincts and don't run away from your inner voice when it is hinting to you that something is wrong. Trust yourself to keep your identity intact. Trust yourself to know that you will do what is needed to meet your needs and desires. Trust yourself to know that if, despite all your efforts, the relationship is not working, you can leave with dignity and without losing any part of yourself.

Trusting yourself is almost a certain way of eliminating feelings of insecurity. So, work on building self-trust.

And finally, build self-confidence and self-esteem. These are useful elements that help in countering your insecurity. Poor self-esteem means you need outside validation to feel good about yourself. In the long run, this approach will not hold much water. Instead, look within and be your own inspiration by building self-esteem and self-confidence. Another chapter in this book deals with this crucial element in detail.

Managing Relationship Anxiety - Healthy Boundaries, Couple Conflicts, and Insecurity

Remind yourself that no one is perfect, and we all have our weaknesses and vulnerabilities. However, being perfect is not necessary to be in a happy relationship. Take your attention off of other people's opinions and focus on yourself and your needs. Insecurity will fly out of the window.

Chapter Four

Managing Your Inner Critic

The story I am going to narrate in this chapter is an episode that resulted in a hasty decision because I gave in to the power of my inner critic voice. After a few failed and unhappy relationships, I was in one where I was actually satisfied and happy. I am going to call this partner Jordan to ensure privacy and for ease of reference.

Sarah is definitely a part of this story too. She is like a lifeline who followed me through my entire recovery process, making herself available to me 24/7, sometimes physically, and sometimes, virtually. I could reach out to Sarah, and she would be there to console me, make me laugh, or use any other method to get me back on track.

Jordan and I had a great relationship going. He was not much of a talker, though. Looking back, I realized he was actually everything I wanted in a partner. He was loving, caring, genuine, honest, and had a great sense of humor, although I took a while to understood his subtle wit.

Anxious in Love

It was not that I was not aware of what a great partner I had in Jordan. In fact, my fear was that he was too good to be true. Thanks to my self-doubt created by my inner critic voice, I worried that I got excessively attached to him, and if, for any reason whatsoever, the relationship was to break apart, I will never be able to get over the pain. It's not that I was making a great success in overcoming the negative effects of my earlier failed relationships. I was riddled with self-doubt, fear, and anxiety, constantly worrying as to how long this wonderful relationship would last.

Each time my inner critic voice told me, "You don't deserve him. He is going to leave you for someone better," I would turn on a nasty and unpleasant behavior at the slightest provocation that Jordan provided me with. Often, there would hardly be a provocation, and still, I would pounce on him, call him names, and accuse him of things he was completely incapable of doing. It was like I wanted this relationship to fail so that my inner critic voice could say, "I told you so!"

I would pick up fights on the silliest of mistakes, and one particular incident is worthy of mention at this point. We were having dinner at a fancy restaurant. That day was particularly difficult for me because we had bumped into his ex-girlfriend on the way to the restaurant. And boy! Was she sexy! She looked gorgeous in a tight-fitting gown with a side cut that showed off her sexy, excellently toned legs. Jordan and I were waiting for the traffic signal to turn green so that we could cross the road.

There was this beautiful chick waiting on the other side to come over to our side. I was grudgingly and enviously admiring her flat stomach and well-toned leg muscles when I realized that she was waving at me. I was taken aback for an instant, wondering if I knew her from somewhere when it suddenly struck me that she was waving wildly at Jordan. She was signaling to him to stay where he was, while she crossed over to meet us.

The worst part was Jordan was responding equally happily to her wave and held both of us back, waiting for this absolute stunner of a woman to walk across and give him a huge hug. By the way, I could've sworn then that Jordan hugged her back with as much enthusiasm.

The feeling of jealousy hit me instantaneously. My mind raced crazily with wild thoughts that Jordan was having an affair with this beautiful girl, and he was going to leave me anytime soon. Maybe he planned this dinner at the fancy restaurant to break the news to me as gently as he could.

After that tight hug, she looked at him and said, "Hey, handsome! How have you been?" And I swear her eyes had a bitchy glint in them as she turned to me expecting to be introduced. Jordan actually blushed at her compliment, and he stared at her as if he hadn't seen a beautiful woman ever before in his life! I was appalled, and the green monster dug its tentacles deep into my heart and mind.

Jordan did the introductions, "Hi Alicia! Great to see you after so many years! Meet my girlfriend, Amanda. And Amanda, meet Alicia, a great friend." Alicia added a wee bit too quickly for my liking, "And ex-girlfriend! We had a great one going, right, Jordan?"

We shook hands, and she smiled sweetly (a bit too sweet, almost sickly sweet, warned my inner critic voice) at me. I smiled back a little wanly because by now, my anxiety pangs had hit, and I was sweating thinking of all the negative possibilities of us meeting Jordan's ex-girlfriend just like that.

"Don't didn't believe in coincidences," warned my voice. And my anxiety pangs made it even more difficult to try and convince that this meeting was nothing more than a coincidence.

They spoke for a while, excitedly, and happily. The voice told me, "Look at Jordan! Have you ever seen him as excited and happy as he seems now with Alicia? I think this is the girl he is going to dump you for!" They recalled their fun days together. They were talking about one particularly great party they had gone on a private beach belonging to some rich friend. They were laughing uproariously cracking old jokes. It was a very long time before both of them finally realized that I was there too.

They both said together, "Sorry, Amanda! We just forgot you were there." My voice said, "Even nature seems to accept them as a great couple. They even seem to say things in perfect synchronization."

I was so raving jealous at that moment that I could have killed her if given an opportunity. But, I smiled sweetly and said, "No problem at all." After a few more minutes of talking, we parted ways, but only after Jordan and Alicia exchanged mobile numbers and promised to be in touch. She even gave him a goodbye kiss on his cheek, making Jordan blush even more than before. This one incident was enough to set my jealousy meter aflutter. I began to think Jordan was nothing more than Peter Pan, and he would leave me soon.

Then we went to cross the road and get on the pavement on the other side of the traffic signal to the fancy restaurant for dinner. But nothing fancy was happening in my own head. I was only picturizing the day when he would say, "I am sorry, Amanda! But I don't think this is working out for us. I think it's break-up time for us. It was great as long as we were together. But now it's time to move on. I am sure you will find your 'right one' just like I found mine."

I imagined the pain of the heartbreak using all my previous experiences and blowing them out of proportion in my mind. I didn't have the courage to withstand that pain, I told myself. I had to take control before something I cannot handle takes control of me. I started the exercise of distancing myself from Jordan as a way of cushioning the pain from that day onwards. The dinner date at the fancy restaurant was a complete disaster to start with, and all because of me.

He asked, "What would you like to drink?"

I replied, "I'll just have sparkling water!"

He said, "What! I thought we could have champagne."

I replied, "Nah! I am not in the mood to drink!"

He asked, "What would you like to eat?"

I replied in a monotonous voice, "Maybe a green salad!"

I had switched myself off so strongly that the poor man stood no chance to do anything. I simply kept him at a distance to save myself the pain of heartbreak. I closed my heart thinking that I didn't warm it up, then when the coldness comes, I will not feel the pain.

It didn't take more than a couple of days for me to say what I imagined he would say to me. In fact, I didn't even have the decency to tell him anything to his face. One day after he left for his office, I called in sick, packed my bags, and left his apartment, leaving a note with nothing more than, "I want to break up, Jordan. It's not working between us." I left him no forwarding address.

Sarah tried her best to patch up things between us. She kept hammering me to tell her what exactly happened because Jordan couldn't think of any reason for my weird behavior. He was devastated, Sarah told me. I thought he was just pretending to be devastated. In truth, he would have been happy that I did the difficult work for him by choosing to leave him so that he could be free to follow a woman more beautiful than me. I told Sarah not to fall for his 'acting skills' of being devastated. I was not ready to listen to reason.

Much later, when I realized my own folly in this episode, I thought that Jordan would have been truly pained at my sudden, inexplicable departure from his life. Sadly, I was paid for my insensitivity. Sarah told me that he met another girl soon enough and was happily married to her now. And no, it was not Alicia; that was apparently just a fling and nothing more to both of them. So, that is my experience of how I allowed my anxiety to make decisions that were counterproductive to my own happiness and joy. I wish I had paid less attention to or countered the baseless fears that my inner critic voice filled my head with.

Falling in love is wonderful, undoubtedly. But, it also has the power to challenge us in numerous, unexpected ways. The more we love and value someone in our lives, the more we stand to lose, if anything were to happen to the relationship. We are scared of getting hurt. This fear affects us at both our conscious and subconscious levels.

Interestingly, nearly all of us have a fear of intimacy, and ironically, we get this fear when we are on the verge of getting exactly what we want. The fear of intimacy comes precisely at that time when we experience love in its deepest form. When we get what we have desired all our lives, that feeling is unfamiliar and strange, and the fear of intimacy raises its ugly head.

There are many causes of relationship anxiety. One of the most debilitating factors is the impact of the inner critic voice.

Understanding the Voice of the Inner Critic

We all have a mean coach inside our own heads whose primary aim is to criticize anything and everything we do. It gives us bad advice, discourages us from trying to achieve our best, and enjoys fueling our fears and vulnerabilities. The inner critic voice tells us things like:

- You are not good enough for your partner.

- You don't deserve your spouse.

- You have no special gift.

- Why should anyone love you at all?

- The man who appears decent cannot be trusted.

- You will fail, just like always.

Managing Your Inner Critic

- Your partner doesn't love or care for you.

The power of your inner critic voice should not be underestimated, especially because of its ability to make you think the worst of yourself. It promotes self-hate, which, in turn, drives us to hate and fears others around us, even those who genuinely care for us. The inner critic voice promotes suspicious thoughts, hostility, and paranoia, more often unnecessarily than needed.

This inner critic voice does everything in its power to undermine our happiness and fill our minds with relationship anxiety. When we allow this voice to rule us, we become its slave, and instead of enjoying the relationship, we end up spending our time and energy on worrying about nebulous ideas that may never reach fruition. Consequently, we end up behaving in destructive ways, including making immature and hateful comments about our partners and take on a parental or childish attitude when interacting with them.

For example, suppose your partner had an all-nighter at work one day. You are alone at home with an almost endless night ahead of you. Your inner critic voice is quite likely to start its work, considering that you are alone and are not likely to be able to talk to anyone at night. This voice starts by asking you questions like:

- I wonder where he or she is right now!

- Is he (or she) really at work?

- Didn't he (or she) say that a big project just got over and the chances of staying late at work are low just a month ago?

- Can you really believe what he (or she) is saying?

- Does your partner prefer being away from you?

- Does he (or she) always find an excuse not to come home?

All these negative thoughts snowball into an avalanche in your mind, and by the time your partner comes back, you are filled with anger and resentment, which, in turn, trigger feelings of insecurity and paranoia. You react angrily, or worse still, coldly to your partner. After repeated such instances, a day will come when your partner will get fed up with you and leave you.

If you notice, you have created an exact trap that you have been trying to avoid. The primary culprit behind this self-fulfilling prophecy is your own inner critic voice. And all because you didn't find the courage or will to fight back against the inner critic voice that distorted your perceptions and colored your thoughts, driving you down the path of relationship anxiety.

We are all capable of handling our rejections and hurts from our previous experiences; only we found the right way to manage and counter the effects of the inner critic voice that terrorizes and creates imaginative catastrophes out of reality. This powerful, terrorizing voice that continuously speaks to us is capable of rousing anxiety about non-existent issues in relationship dynamics.

The worst thing about this voice is its capability to make us feel worthless and undeserving. Therefore, when we experience real things like unblemished and true gestures based on love and affection from a potential suitor, this voice will find its way into our heads and tell us that we don't deserve this person. The voice is like that cynical classmate or roommate who tells you, "Don't get into this mess. You cannot handle the consequences. Put up your guard, and don't reveal your vulnerabilities to anyone. Remember the pain from the previous time? Do you want to experience that agony again?"

It is extremely easy to fall into this fear- and insecurity-based trap set up by your inner critic voice.

We quickly fall back into the comfort zones we have created for ourselves to avoid this fear. In an existing relationship like in the one used in the above illustration, this kind of anxiety invariably drives us to become clingy, desperate, and possessive towards our partner.

Some of us, in such situations, choose to retreat from the relationship in the hope of keeping the pain of rejection and hurt at bay, and we become aloof, guarded, and distant. Our current behavior is highly influenced by the attachment pattern styles we adopted during our childhood days. The subject of attachment pattern styles is handled in a different chapter in this book.

Relationship Anxiety Thought Patterns Perpetuated by the Inner Critic

Each of us has our own thought patterns formed from earlier life experiences, in which the inner critic voice tends to harness its power. Attitudes of our caretakers in our childhood, sexual stereotypes we have been exposed to, and many other factors give power to our inner critic voice, thereby coloring our perceptions and thoughts. Yet, there are some common types of relationship anxiety thought patterns used by the inner critic voice for many of us. Let us look at some of the common types.

Critical thoughts about our relationships could be one or more of the following:

- All human beings are designed to get hurt in the end, no matter what we do to prevent it.

- Relationships are not meant to succeed.

Thought patterns used by the inner critic voice to hate yourself could be in the form of:

- Don't get excessively attached to her.

- You will never find anyone who understands you.

- He is too good for you.

- She doesn't really care for you.

- As soon as he knows about your weakness, he will leave you.

- It is better to be lonely than try to find love and fail.

- You have no control over yourself.

- Don't ever show your vulnerability to anyone. Else, you will end up getting hurt.

- It is all your fault.

Thought patterns driven by our inner critic voice towards our partners could be something like the ones mentioned here:

- All men are selfish, mean, unreliable, and insensitive.

- All women are indirect, needy, and clingy.

- He cares only for his profession, games, and friends.

- She is too career-oriented to focus on our family.

- She gets way too excited about everything.

- He was a flirt, even in college. Therefore, he must be cheating on me now too.

- He cannot be trusted.

- She just cannot do anything without crying.

Effects of Thought Patterns On Relationship Anxiety

These thought patterns affect the way we handle your relationships because they form one of the primary causes of relationship anxiety. So, how does the inner critic voice affect your behavior and your relationships?

Rejecting - Saying no or rejecting your partner is one of the most common defensive mechanisms used by people with relationship anxiety. They think, "Let me say no before he or she says no so that I can save myself from the pain of being rejected." Another form of rejection is aloofness. You tend to take a cold attitude towards your partner in the hope of protecting yourself from getting hurt. This kind of behavior is sure to drive your partner away or even stir up insecurity in his or her mind, which is again dangerous for the relationship.

Cling - Feelings of anxiety are powerful enough for you to feel the need to cling excessively to our partners. Your personality could undergo a drastic change from being a strong, independent person to one who feels jealous, insecure, and incapable of engaging in independent activities of your own.

Control - Relationship anxiety can have two facets; one in which the affected person becomes clingy and desperate or takes the other extreme side of trying to dominate and control your partner. You could set unreasonable expectations from your partner and draw up rules that don't make any sense. You could use these controlling strategies to allay your own fears and insecurities. Of course, in the long run, such kinds of dominating behavior are bound to drive your partner away from you.

Retreat - The inner critic voice is so powerful that it can drive us to retreat from ourselves and our true needs. We begin to believe that we don't deserve anything, and therefore, we must retreat from the field of love and relationships. Worse still, some people tend to retreat into a fantasy world of love and intimacy even as they maintain a shallow relationship in real life. Such a retreating attitude results in people putting form and pretense over substance resulting in superficial relationships.

Punish - Sometimes, relationship anxiety driven by the inner critic voice pushes to take a punishing attitude towards our partner. We tend to get aggressive in our behavior, yelling and screaming at our partner because of the fear instilled in us by our inner critic voice.

Withhold - Another common effect of heeding the inner critic voice is to withhold your feelings and fears from your partner. We tend to withhold our feelings of love and affection as well, which makes us come across as being indifferent towards our partner, which, of course, will drive him or her away from you.

How to Tame Your Inner Critic

The private conversations you have with yourself frequently mediated by your inner critic voice can be a huge deterrent or a powerful stepping stone for success in all aspects of your life, including relationships. It is imperative that you prevent yourself from giving in to the negative thoughts of your inner critic voice, considering that these thoughts have an uncanny power to become self-fulfilling prophecies. So, learn to tame your inner critic voice and take control of your thoughts.

Become aware of your thoughts - We get so accustomed to our own thoughts that it becomes an ingrained habit to listen to them without considering the underlying messages that send us. Most often, our thoughts are exaggerated, disproportionate, and highly biased. Pay attention to your thoughts and remind yourself that not all your thoughts are really true.

Avoid ruminating - It is natural for most of us to replay unpleasant and embarrassing events and experiences repeatedly in our heads. This process is referred to as ruminating, and we do it in the hope that things will appear less unpleasant than it actually was. Or we could do it simply as a witch-hunting process against ourselves.

Whatever is the reason for ruminating, catch yourself when you are in this situation, and remind yourself not to waste time and energy on it. Repeating unpleasant thoughts in your head adds no value to your life. On the contrary, your inner critic voice gets undue power from these valueless thoughts. Each time you find yourself ruminating, shift your thought process into a problem-solving mode, and try and find lessons you can imbibe from those life experiences.

Treat yourself as you would treat your best friend - If your best friend came to you for advice, what would you tell him or her? Would you make any of these statements to a friend?

- What a stupid thing to do!

- You cannot really get into a relationship because you are unworthy of it.

- No one really likes you.

Of course not! You would try and explain to your best friend how things really stand and how he or she can get better, right? Speak to yourself in the same way. Remind yourself that you are your best friend. Apply the same words of encouragement as you would use to encourage your best friend.

Look behind the thoughts and examine the underlying evidence and facts - For example, suppose you are on a first date with a potential partner, and you really like what you see in him or her. Now, your inner critic voice will raise its ugly head and try to dissuade you from taking the next step in the relationship, maybe even a harmless second date. At this juncture, stop your inner critic voice and examine the facts underlying those thoughts.

Why is your inner critic voice trying to dissuade you? Is it because of the painful memories of a previous relationship? If yes, what happened then? What are the chances the same will happen now? Can you do something to prevent a recurrence of the previous events/experiences?

In this way, you can counter your inner critic voice by examining the underlying evidence between the criticisms and the holding-back mechanisms. As you look for answers to such questions objectively, you will find the way to discern between thoughts that require to be heeded and those that are merely causing you distress and building relationship anxiety.

Replace critical thoughts in your head with specific and detailed statements - Again, let us take an example. Suppose your inner critic voice is telling you, "You always end up in pain." Now, reword this highly generalized statement with specific example(s) of when and how you ended up in pain.

After such an examination, you are quite likely to come up with more balanced statements that go with something like, "When Susan left me without even a goodbye, I felt hurt. But, it is also true that she had tried to warn me about things that upset her, and I did nothing about it." A more balanced outlook of your behavior is bound to come out when you don't get carried away by the generalized critical statements your inner critic voice tends to throw at you.

Look at the worst-case scenario - Often, visualizing something to end in a catastrophe can be quite tempting because it gives a reason to stay in your comfort zone. In reality, imagined worst-case scenarios are very rare. Frequently, even the worst that really happens is far less ominous than your imagined catastrophes.

Let us take the case of a first date going on reasonably well, and your potential partner asks you for a second case. Your inner critic voice is telling you not to accept it. Now, stop yourself and visualize the worst that can happen if you agree for a second date. For example, would it be that the relationship does not go into the third date? If yes, can you not prepare yourself to handle such a situation? After all, you continue your life as before, right?

Therefore, don't allow your inner critic voice to prepare for and handle worst-case scenarios.

Balance acceptance with improvement - There is a huge difference between the negative thoughts of your inner critic voice telling you that you are worthless, and you are reminding yourself that it is possible to work towards improvement and succeed too. There is nothing wrong with having flaws, and when you accept and embrace your flaws with humility, this is when your inner critic voice loses its power.

Therefore, it is vital that you accept yourself as you are, including warts and all, and then work towards improving yourself. As you get better with your efforts, you will find it increasingly easy to ward off the negativity of your inner critic voice. That is the power of balancing acceptance with improvement.

Your conversations with yourself can make or break your ability to handle relationships by overcoming relationship anxiety issues. Your inner critic voice is essential to help you point out your flaws. But, beyond that, its effects are debilitating and counterproductive to your growth as an individual.

Therefore, listen to your inner critic voice, but only up to a certain point. After that, you must find ways to counter its negative impact and move ahead in your life.

Chapter Five

Understanding Attachment Styles

Attachment styles refer to the pattern of bonds we create in our relationships. The different types of attachment styles are described in detail in this chapter. But before we go to the details of various attachment styles and how they are formed and affect the relationships you create; I have to narrate to you the story of my personal attachment style.

I learned much later that I am a typical example of a person with a dismissive-avoidant attachment style. It is a style that I seemed to have developed in my childhood. It has something to do with the way I was raised, it seems. My parents were busy with their professions and so hardly had time for me. I couldn't recall moments of hugs and love, the ones I see on ad campaigns speaking of parental care and love.

It's not that they did not provide for me. They gave me a good education and made sure I never wanted for anything that I needed. But, both of them were so busy and caught up in their own jobs that they didn't have the time and energy to show great concern for me.

For example, I recall an incident when I was 5-6 years old. That memory had uncannily stayed in my head. It stayed there until I was able to face it and handle all the feelings associated with it with the professional help of a qualified and trained counselor. Again, it was Sarah who helped me see the need to take professional help in my case.

When I was around 5 or 6 years of age, I had gotten hurt really badly. I was playing with the neighbor kids and had fallen off the first-floor parapet wall. When I screamed in pain, my mother came running out, and instead of holding and comforting me, she shouted at me for being careless.

I remember her words even now, "I have such an important project deadline to meet! Now is the time you choose to fall and hurt yourself? Can't you look after yourself?"

Tears of pain sting my eyes even now when I recall my mother's words. Of course, I have made peace with her now, and we are a good daughter-mother duo currently. But, such incidents in my childhood seem to have forced me to create the dismissive-avoidant attachment style.

Understanding Attachment Styles

I believed that if I stay away from others and don't attach myself to people excessively and don't show my vulnerabilities to them, then I can avoid the pain of being rejected. This style primarily drove most of my relationships until I learned to overcome it.

After my breakup with Jordan, I was single for a long time as I didn't want to get hurt again. Then, one day, I got introduced to Aaron, an always-smiling and happy-go-lucky guy. He made me laugh so much I couldn't help falling in love with him. Aaron was a nice, jolly person, and had no expectations from me, except to be myself. But my anxiety-based attachment style did little to help me sustain this easy relationship too.

Despite this, both of us did our best to keep it going, and it was a fine experience with Aaron until one day, his overly happy-go-lucky nature brought out the worst of my dismissive-avoidant attachment style. All his friends, and he had a huge social circle, thanks to his gregarious nature, organized a grand party for his birthday. Of course, I had to be there too because I was his girlfriend.

I reluctantly got dressed for the party and arrived at the venue with Aaron in tow. As soon as we made the entrance, the party got off to a ruckus start. Everyone cheered for Aaron and sang loudly for him, and things appeared to have gotten off superbly. I also began to slowly open up and enjoy myself.

Many of his friends were like him, happy and jolly always, cracking jokes and making everyone laugh. It was a good party indeed until I saw how much Aaron was enjoying himself. To me, it seemed he was surrounded only by girls. I hardly could see any man laughing at Aaron's jokes as much as the women were.

And the women who were surrounding him were great looking. Not that I was any less good-looking. But, still, my self-doubt nagged me, and my attachment style took over my behavior. I began to worry that he was scouting for a potential partner so that he could get away from me. Anyway, I was not really his kind of girl, happy and laughing always.

I could be quite morose and totally become silent if I wanted to. Moreover, the worry that if I spoke a lot, then my vulnerabilities will come to the forefront, and people will scold or shout at me prevented me from being more social and gregarious. I was filled with dread imagining my house becoming empty of laughter after Aaron moves out. The emptiness in my imagination filled my heart with anxiety-laden fear of losing him and then having to deal with the pain of loss.

Understanding Attachment Styles

Aaron looked at me from across the room and smiled, which could have meant anything. But, I chose to believe that his smile had a tinge of mockery. He seemed to say, "Can you see how easy it is for me to leave you? Can you behave in ways that will make me want to stay with you instead of going away with one of these women?"

Now I look back and know that these thoughts had the same meaning as the words my mother used to tell me, that I have to work hard to earn her love and attention because she had other important things to do. I did the same thing with Aaron that I did with my mother. I chose to take a dismissive attitude towards Aaron so that I didn't have to take the pain of losing him when he chooses to move out, just like how I chose the attachment style to keep the pain of not getting my parent's love at bay.

My increasingly detached behavior made it difficult for Aaron to have a happy relationship. It was not very long after the day of the party that he chose to break up with me.

He said, "I think this is not working for us, right?"

I said, "Oh! Really? I don't know. I thought everything was fine." There was a clearly dismissive tone to my voice.

He said, "No, everything is not fine, and you are holding back something."

I replied, "No, I am not holding back anything. I am happy. I don't know why you are not."

He said, "I've tried hard enough, and now I cannot go on anymore. I want to leave."

I looked at him and said, "Okay! No problem. You can leave whenever you want. Just try and choose a day when I am not around because the dust created while you move your things out gives me an allergy!"

The horrifying look on his Aaron's face matched in intensity at the pain in my heart. And yet, I chose dismissiveness over any other kind of behavior because I believed this was the only way to deal with such situations. I had no option but to look after myself and not lean on anyone for help.

Attachment styles in adults are used as reference points to describe patterns of attachment demonstrated in romantic relationships. Attachment styles in general refer to the different methods used by people to interact and behave in relationships. During childhood, attachment styles are typically centered on the child and his or her caregiver or parent.

Understanding Attachment Styles

In psychology, an attachment can be defined as the emotional relationship involving the exchange of love, care, and comfort between two people. John Bowlby, a famous 20th-century British psychologist and psychoanalyst is credited with doing extensive research on the subject of attachment styles. According to Bowlby, attachment styles developed in early childhood have a significant impact on adult life, especially while establishing romantic relationships.

John Bowlby also theorized that there are four distinctive traits of attachment developed during childhood by the child towards the caregiver. These four traits are secure base, safe haven, proximity maintenance, and separation distress. Here is a brief explanation of each of these characteristics:

• Secure base - The attachment figure becomes the center of support for the child from where he or she explores the surrounding world and environment.

• Safe haven - Allowing the child to return to the security of the attachment figure for safety and comfort, especially during times of distress and fear.

• Proximity maintenance - The desire to be as close to the attachment figure as possible.

- Separation distress - This refers to the stress and anxiety felt in the absence of the attachment figure.

The attachment style theory is based on the following three tenets:

When children are brought up with the confidence that their attachment figure is close at hand and will be there for them, they are less likely to experience fear and insecurity than those children who don't have access to this confidence.

This confidence is built during the critical period of growth, starting from infancy moving into childhood and finally into adolescence. The life experiences, including attachment styles and expectations from people in relationships, learned during these phases of life, remain more or less unchanged right through adulthood.

These expectations from relationships are directly connected to experiences. So, a person who has had a caregiver (or parent) who has given him or her the confidence of being available in times of need will continue to expect this even from their romantic partners. Attachment styles are established in early childhood periods and become more or less our model for relationships in adulthood. However, these attachment patterns picked up from childhood are

Understanding Attachment Styles

not cast in stone. They can undergo changes depending on our adult experiences as well.

Our attachment style impacts everything in our relationships right from partner selection to how we maintain it even to end it (if it happens). Therefore, identifying our attachment style will help us understand our weaknesses and strengths in relationships.

To give you an example, if you are a person with an anxious attachment style, then it is likely that you feel the urge to be close to your partner at all times if you can have your needs for love and affection met. You constantly need reassurance that the relationship is going in the right direction. Driven by this perceived need, you tend to find a partner who likes being alone and is quite difficult to connect with.

Another example to illustrate how your attachment style could affect the choice of your partner. Suppose you had an avoidant attachment style, which means you pretend to be distant. This approach is based on your belief that your need to connect with another human being can be met only if you show or demonstrate that you don't have this need. Such people tend to choose partners who are possessive and/or demand excessive attention.

Therefore, typically, we tend to look for partners who confirm our attachment models and our belief in these styles. If we developed an insecure attachment style in our childhood, we tend to seek or project a similar pattern in relationships we build as adults, even if these styles end up with outcomes that hurt us. Let us look at the four common attachment styles that most of us typically fit into.

Secure Attachment Style

The characteristics of a secure attachment style can be summarized as follows:

• Children who develop a secure attachment style tend to become visibly upset and worried when their caregiver leaves and are visibly happy when the caregivers return.

• When children are frightened, they tend to seek comfort and security from their caregivers.

• Children of this type generally accept any form of contact offered by parents and also return positive behavior to their caregiver.

• Children with this attachment style can be handled by or comforted by others only to a certain extent. But, they clearly prefer the comfort of known and familiar caregivers.

- Children who developed secure attachment styles tend to be more empathetic as they reach adolescence and adulthood.

- Also, such children tend to be less aggressive, less disruptive, and more mature than those who develop any of the other three styles.

Adults with secure attachment styles are likely to have lasting and trusting relationships. They usually have high self-esteem and don't have issues sharing their problems and vulnerabilities with their partners. Also, these people have no issues seeking social support when they feel uncertain or scared.

People with a secure attachment working model tend to find satisfaction and contentment in their relationships. Children brought up with this attachment style view their parents as a secure base from where they can go out into the external world, explore it to their heart's content, and then return to the secure base.

Adults with this kind of attachment style behave similarly. They feel secure in their romantic relationships and connect well with their partners even as they give themselves and their partners the freedom to move around freely outside the relationship, secure in their belief that the relationship has the power to overcome all obstacles.

Secure adults are there for their partners in times of distress and also don't hesitate to approach their partners for help when they are anxious or worried. When both partners use the secure attachment style as their working model, then the relationship is likely, to be honest, open, and fulfilling. Both feel love for each other even as they happily give freedom to their partners for their personal needs and dreams. The bond between partners with a secure attachment style is usually based on true feelings of love and respect for each other.

Anxious or Preoccupied Attachment Style

People with an anxious attachment style tend to form fantasy and inauthentic relationship bonds with their partners, driven by anxiety, which makes them emotionally hungry. Consequently, they tend to look for sources that can 'satiate' this hunger rather than for true love and respect.

Such people tend to look towards their partners to make them feel complete and secure, driven by feelings of insecurity and anxiety. Their clingy behavior towards their partners is nothing but a reflection of their own anxiety-based fears. Such people tend to become demanding and possessive in a relationship.

Moreover, people with an anxious attachment style tend to interpret their partner's behavior in ways that affirm their own beliefs. For example, if their partner socializes a lot with friends, then they would interpret it as, "I told you, he or she doesn't love me. Soon he or she will leave me. Therefore, I shouldn't trust him or her anymore."

Dismissive Avoidant Attachment Style

People with this kind of attachment style tend to be dismissive of their emotional needs and tend to avoid getting into relationships. Even if they do get into relationships, such people tend to keep their distance from their partners, taking on a seemingly independent behavior, seeking to take care of themselves without help from others.

Children with the avoidant attachment style tend to avoid their parents and caregivers too. They don't really seek comfort or security from their parents and do not show any kind of preference for their caregivers over strangers.

Such people tend to come across as being overly self-seeking and focused on their needs looking for creature comforts of their own and appearing to ignore their partner's needs and desires. This 'pseudo-independent' behavior is an illusion they create, hoping to keep people away from them. And yet, such people tend to deny the importance of loved ones and cannot attach themselves to people easily.

Adults with avoidant attachment styles usually have intimacy issues. They do not invest emotionally in any kind of social or romantic relationship. They are quite unwilling and uncomfortable sharing their thoughts and feelings with others, including their partners.

They have the ability to shut down emotionally during times of distress. In fact, in highly emotional or heated situations, these people can turn off their emotions and be in a non-reactive state of mind. If, for example, their partner screams at them and says, "I am going to leave you," they are likely to turn around and say, "Do it. I don't care!"

The unfortunate thing is that such people are the ones who suffer the most. They handle the deepest fears through an attitude of dismissiveness and avoidance. They would hide their fears for fear of being hurt if they showed their vulnerabilities.

Ambivalent or Disorganized Attachment Style

People with this kind of attachment style tend to live in an ambivalent state, continuously shifting their fears from being too distant or too close to their partners. They want to avoid demonstrating their vulnerabilities and feelings but find it difficult to do so. They can neither run away from their emotions nor find the courage to talk openly and honestly about their fears. Driven by this constant stress, such people are likely to experience emotional storms more frequently than others.

Children who develop an ambivalent attachment style tend to behave warily with strangers and get extremely distressed with parents or caregivers leave them. Also, these children don't get easily comforted even when parents or caregivers return to them.

Adults with ambivalent attachment styles tend to be reluctant to get close to their partners. They are constantly anxious that their partners don't love them and will leave them. When relationships end, these people tend to get highly distraught. Considering that they are hesitant to get close to people, their relationship status is in a state of flux as they have frequent breakups. Their partners also find it difficult to connect with them, driven by their cold and distant behavior.

Romantic relationships of such people tend to be highly dramatic, with frequent highs and lows. As they struggle with intimacy issues, they also have to manage their fears of abandonment. They cling to their partners when they feel unwanted and rejected and tended to feel trapped in close, intimate situations.

The attachment style you developed as a child with your caregivers and/or parents need not define you as an adult today. Identify your current attachment style so that you see what is causing you anxiety and preventing you from having fulfilling and meaningful relationships. And then, you can find ways to overcome these issues and learn to give up anxiety in love.

The Usefulness of Seeking Professional Help

Relationship anxiety, attachment, styles, fear of abandonment, fear of loneliness, fear of getting hurt, etc. are all painful and complex elements of a relationship. All of these elements need to be addressed and problems, if any, resolved as soon as possible lest they fester into an incurable state.

Using the services of a trained and qualified therapist can be very useful to deal with anxiety in love. Therapists can help you and your partner get through anxiety in the following ways:

- They will help you identify and understand your feelings and emotions and the underlying causes.

- They will help both of you understand each other's feelings and the underlying issues.

- They will help you with different techniques to handle pressure and anxiety and how to calm your frayed nerves.

The best thing about seeking professional help is that it does not have to be in the long-term. Even one session can make a difference in the way you deal with anxiety and your relationship. You can then take it on from there.

Chapter Six

Harnessing the Power of Positivity

One of the first elements that helped me significantly in overcoming anxiety in love is the power of positive thinking. Thanks to Sarah's timely intervention, she taught me different ways to try and counter negative thoughts and focus more on positive thoughts. I have listed all the ideas I used to improve the power of positive thinking in my life and believe me; it worked like magic. Here is a simple story that reflects the magic that the power of positive thinking can create, if only you have faith and persist in your efforts.

I was slowly getting over the fear of relationships. I went out and met more guys and worked hard at overcoming my personal problems and issues so that they don't come in the way of creating beautiful relationships with other people. After multiple first dates with many men, I finally found a great connection with Edward, a bartender at a pub.

Incidentally, I met him while I was waiting for one of my dates to turn up. Luckily for me, the date didn't turn up for some reason. But, unlike the previous time when I had driven myself crazy thinking that my date had peeked in through the window, saw the 'ugly me,' and left without coming, I was far more relaxed and happy, thanks to my efforts at keeping negative thoughts at bay.

I ordered a second drink telling myself that I will enjoy the quiet evening even if my date doesn't turn up. The bartender handed over the drink and said, "It's nice to see people who can be happy and content in their own company." I was piqued by this statement and looked up to see the man who handed over my drink. A pair of twinkling blue eyes smiled at me. It was impossible not to return that kind of smile.

We got talking, and he would keep finding his way back whenever he didn't have an order to fulfill. We laughed at many things and realized we shared a lot in common, including the disinterest in baseball. When I heard he was not interested in baseball, I was truly bowled over because I was still to meet an American who didn't like baseball.

I jokingly asked him, "Really? Don't you like baseball? That's hard to believe. Are you sure you are not using that as a pick-up line?"

His eyes twinkled again as he replied, "I am glad you think of it as a pick-up line. But no, I wasn't doing so."

We laughed together at this and continued our conversation. I stayed at the bar until it was closing time. By then, we had exchanged names and phone numbers. He walked out with me after closing the bar and hailed a taxi for me too. Soon, we met at a party and realized we even had a common friend. The party (where we met for the second time) is when things got serious between us, and we started a relationship.

It was a great one, perhaps, the best one in a very long time. My anxiety again played its part to put me on edge, making me wonder how long this will last. But this time, I was ready for these negative thoughts. One particular day is worth mentioning here.

Edward and I had moved in together, and everything was going nice. Yes, we did have our fights. But, somehow, we managed to keep our conflicts at tolerable and workable levels. Then one day, a lot of events happened that threatened to flood my heart and mind with negativity.

First, when I woke up, Edward had already left for the day with a note that said, "Sorry, babe! Need to rush somewhere, will be late too. You have a great day and see you tomorrow." That's it! No explanation as to where he went and why he wouldn't be there with me for my birthday. In fact, I had planned to take a day's leave from the office to spend time with Edward. And now this.

Anyway, I decided to see that maybe this is for the good of everyone. I had a big deadline coming up, and taking a day off might not have been a wise choice. So, I got ready and went to my workplace. As soon as I reached, my computer crashed, and all the data for my upcoming project was lost. I was shattered and actually scared of what my boss will say.

But I didn't give in to my negative thoughts. Instead, I focused on how I can get my computer back in its working condition. I went to the IT guys and promised them a special treat if they managed to get my computer up and running in the next two hours. I had my best smile on when I approached them with my problem. The IT guys (two of them) were infected with my positivity and decided to take up the challenge.

They were not only able to get my computer up and running within the promised time but were also able to retrieve all my lost records! I was thrilled, of course, and as promised, I took the young boys out to lunch to a fancy place. Their joy knew no bounds because such a lunch was a first for them.

After lunch, my problems didn't cease. My deadline was preponed by a couple of days, but the project was due by the end of that day! Again, thanking my stars for giving me the wisdom to come to the office today instead of moping at home, I got to work and completed the work. I have to mention that the negativity of my boss didn't help at all. I simply persisted against his angry and frustrated attitude. Perhaps, his girlfriend did something to him just like Edward did to me this morning. Poor chap!

Another thing that kept me on hooks the entire day was that Edward was not answering his phone at all. I tried calling him at least 20 times to no avail. I told myself that this attitude was quite unlike his natural self. He must be busy with something, and that's why he is not responding to my calls and messages.

Finally, the difficult day ended. The project was submitted, and I took the subway home totally exhausted and waiting to jump into bed. My stomach was growling from hunger. The lunch with the IT boys was my last meal, and I realized I was famished. My phone calls to Edward were still unanswered.

Harnessing the Power of Positivity

I reached the apartment and turned the key in the lock, and saw my home was still in darkness. However, I could hear the strains of my favorite song playing in the background. And hazy light coming from the kitchen-cum-dining area. I walked carefully, wondering if there was a thief at home when suddenly from behind, Edward caught me and gave me one of the warmest hugs I could have had in my entire life, all the while singing, "Happy birthday to you!"

He had organized the most romantic candle-lit dinner ever for me. And I knew my attempts at positive thoughts paid off in ways that defied my imagination.

"Is your glass half-empty or half-full?" What is your answer to this question? How you answer this timeless question gauges your outlook on life. Do you focus more on the empty part of the glass or the filled part of the glass? Do you have an optimistic or pessimistic outlook?

Positivity attracts positivity, which means to say the more you build your positivity, the more it will be cover all aspects of your life. Referred to as the law of attraction, this concept is based on the idea that what you desire and live by will attract more of the same thing.

If you are anxious, cynical, and insecure, you are likely to attract negativity, and the reverse is also true. Which means to say if you are filled with negativity, you will attract anxiety, cynicism, insecurity, and other negative things into your life.

A classic example is the legendary story of Walt Disney. Did you know that before he became famous, he was fired by the editor of a top US newspaper because he was not creative enough? If he had believed in this negative feedback, the world would have lost the magic of Disney.

Instead of being bogged down by negativity, Walt Disney believed he had what he takes for success and simply persisted in his efforts. The universe gave him his desire. That is the power of positive thinking.

What is positive thinking? It is the mental and emotional attitude that focuses on the good and positive aspects that benefit the thinker. Positive thinking drives you to anticipate good health, success, happiness, and joy and also drives you to achieve these elements through persistent hard work.

Despite all the benefits of positive thinking, the human mind seems to be designed for negativity. We seem to be predisposed to negative things. We tend to focus more on dark emotions, including sadness, depression, anger, pain, insecurity, disappointment, etc. than we do on happy emotions like gratitude, contentment, joy, etc. Even when we reflect on our lives, we tend to focus on things that gave pain and forget about things that gave us joy and happiness.

Give yourself a test. Before leaving for work, look at two pictures, one of a cute little puppy and another one that depicts a violent crime. You will notice that, as the day progresses, you are likely to forget the picture of the cute little puppy and recall the violent crime picture often. And this is when you are consciously doing this activity.

Unconsciously, you might not recall the picture of the puppy even once during the day. But the other one will remain in your mind for a long time. You might even discuss it with your colleagues. It is more or less natural for the human mind to skew towards negativity. However, it is possible to shift this attitude and get your mind to think positive thoughts. And there is a science behind this behavior defined as neuroplasticity.

Neuroplasticity is the ability of the human brain to change and adapt, based on life experiences, our thoughts, and the circumstances we encounter. Also, if these experiences and thoughts are repeated sufficiently, then our brain has the power to make new nerve connections to associate the thoughts and the behavior and/or situation and convert these connections into habits.

For example, if you work in a library and you hate what you are doing, soon you will realize that you despise the sight and smell of books. It is not that you don't like books. You love to read them. But your brain has created connections that connect your hatred for your job to books. This connection turns into a habit, and you will get upset every time you come in contact with books.

So, you see your emotions become part of you. When we hate something, our brain connects that hatred to everything related to that something. The good thing is that the reverse is also true. If you can change your hatred into love, then too, your brain will make love-based connections, which, in turn, become habits. It is our choices that create good or bad habits.

Therefore, it is possible to train your mind to think positively and create good habits in your life. Consequently, emotions like anxiety and insecurity will find no place in your life.

Positive thinking is not a vague theoretical concept found only in books. The effects of positive thinking are many, and numerous studies prove its efficacy in the following benefits:

- Lower depression and anxiety rates

- Improved physical and mental well-being which, in turn, has the power to increase your lifespan

- Lowered stress levels

- Improved coping skills during difficult times

While science still has not been able to understand why positive thinking has so many benefits, there is little doubt that if you engage in positive thinking, you can harness the advantages mentioned above and more. Here are some highly implementable ways to train your mind to have positive thoughts.

Gratitude for Positivity

Multiple studies have shown that practicing gratitude makes us happier and less anxious than otherwise. The emotion of gratitude is known to trigger the production and release of dopamine, the happiness hormone believed to be extremely useful in driving out anxiety and negative thoughts.

Gratitude follows the law of attraction. The more you feel grateful, the more elements you will get into your life to increase your feeling of gratitude. So, focus on building a life of gratitude using one or more of the following tips:

Create and maintain a gratitude journal - If you have not already made a gratitude journal, start one today. At the end of each day, make a note of 2-3 things that happened for which you are grateful. Keeping aside some time every day to recall, be grateful for, and record events and people who gave you joy and happiness is a sure-shot way of allowing the powerful element of gratitude to become part of your life.

Recall the bad things that happened in your life - If you want to be grateful for your current life and what you have, then you must recall the times when you didn't have these elements and what it was like without them. Remind yourself how difficult your life was and how far you have come from that point. Compare the present time and the bad times and make a list of the comparative points. This list will be a great place to find many reasons to be grateful for in your present life.

Be aware and conscious of your senses - The five senses available to humans, including the ability to see, feel or touch, taste, smell, and hear are miracles we tend to overlook. If you put your focus back on these senses, you will see there is so much around you to appreciate and feel grateful for.

When you look at the power of the human body and mind through the lens of gratitude, you will realize it is not just a wonderful machine but a gift of nature. You will realize the importance of not taking these seemingly little things for granted.

Practice the 'Naikan' art of self-reflection - 'Naikan' is a structured method of self-reflected rooted and practiced in Japanese culture. It focuses on finding answers to three important life questions, including:

1. What have I got from _____?

2. What have I given to _____?

3. What problems, troubles, and difficulties have I caused?

Watch the words you use - Be conscious of the words you use while talking to people or voicing your thoughts. Words like blessings, abundance, fortunate, fortune, gifts, etc. should take precedence over your inherent goodness. For example, if you have excellent communication skills, then your words to describe yourself should ideally be something like, "I am grateful for the communication skills that were imparted to me by amazing school teachers?"

If you have access to basic food, clothing, and shelter, you must remind yourself to say, "I feel blessed that I have enough not just for myself but can also feed another hungry mouth today." Always focus on what good others have done for you. Even when someone has hurt you in some way, your thoughts for that person should be, "I am grateful to him or her for giving me the opportunity to learn lessons well."

It might be a great idea to make a note of all the negative words you use right through the day. At the end of the day, sit with this list and write one positive alternative against each negative word.

Also, remember that during the initial days of practicing gratitude, you may not really 'feel' it and might be discouraged to give up, thanks to the sense of inauthenticity you are likely to experience. My sincere request to you is to persist in your efforts and not give up. Go through the motions of showing gratitude by saying thank you, making entries in your journal, recalling people and events which have benefited you, etc.

Your persistence will bear fruit. Remember, it takes time for the brain to make new connections and make them so deep that they become a beneficial habit. Be patient with the world around and yourself too. So, start studying your habits, notice those that are detrimental to positive thinking and either alter them or eliminate them to be replaced with good habits that are beneficial for positive thinking.

Take Care of Yourself

Most of us treat self-care as either "taken for granted" or worse still, with disdain. Suppose someone was to ask you, "Do you take care of yourself?" What would you say? Your reply would most probably be, "Of course, I take care of myself!"

Now, the next question from the person would be, "How do you take care of yourself?" This question will stump you because you don't know how to self-care. Now is the time to start.

Self-care is any activity that is deliberately undertaken to take care of your own physical, mental, and emotional health. Self-care is doing something for ourselves that we enjoy. At the end of the self-care activity, our energy levels should be refueled and replenished, not depleted.

Taking care of yourself is not being selfish. On the contrary, it is an act of love towards your loved ones, including your partner. You can add value to a relationship only when you are physically, mentally, and emotionally fit. If any of these three elements is lacking, then you cannot give your full potential to your relationship leading to conflicts and anxiety.

So, where do you start the self-care routine? Start with basics. What do you love to do? Don't get into complex things at this point in time because, as you progress in your path of self-care, you will find your own rhythm. For example, do you love reading? If yes, just set aside time to read something you enjoy.

Start with something as simple as the example mentioned above. Just make sure that when you indulge in the activity, you are completely undisturbed. Let everyone know that you should not be disturbed during that time. Make it a deliberate and conscious act. Announcing it to others increases your commitment to do the activity. Start with one pleasurable activity a day, at least.

Self-care also means to create a 'not to make' list and implement it. Some simple things that should ideally be in your 'not to do' list are:

- Not to look at your phone after 10 pm each night
- Not to miss out daily workouts
- Not to miss regular medical checkups
- Not answering phones while eating

Try this up for 2-3 weeks and see how you feel at the end of the trial period. Remember, like everything else, self-care also requires persistent and diligent practice.

Another way of taking care of yourself is through self-compassion. Treat yourself as you would treat your best friend, especially when you have made a mistake and want to atone for it. Read the chapter on managing your inner critic voice to learn more about this aspect of being kind and compassionate to yourself.

Lead a healthy lifestyle. Taking care of yourself means eating and exercising well to ensure you are physically fit as possible. Try and exercise for at least 30 minutes each day. Exercising is a great way to get out of anxiety and stress because they trigger the production of happy hormones and lift your mood. Avoid junk foods as much as you can and eat wholesome, nutritious meals.

Having a positive approach to life is in no way comparable to burying your head in the sand and ignoring the unpleasant aspects of your life. A positive outlook only means you approach the unpleasant and negative aspects of your life in a productive way. You work towards your goals in the belief that you will get the best outcome because you deserve the best.

Identify crucial areas of change - Identify those areas of your life in which you tend to think more negatively than others. From a relationship anxiety perspective, do you tend to think negatively about your capabilities and the value you bring to the relationship? If yes, you need to start focusing on this area first and be conscious of your negative thoughts voiced often by the inner critic voice. Counter these thoughts suitably using suggestions and recommendations in the chapter on the inner critic voice.

Check your thoughts right through the day - Right through the day, take periodic breaks, and check your thoughts. Each time you catch yourself thinking negatively, put a positive spin to the thought immediately. Here are some examples of how you can convert your negative self-talk to positive ones:

- "I have never done this before," can become, "I think it is a wonderful opportunity to learn something new."

- "This thing is a bit too complicated for my understanding," can become, "Let me see this from a different perspective."

- "I am too tired to get this thing done today," can become, "Let me see how I can reorganize my day to complete this today itself."

- "I don't have sufficient resources to do this," can become, "Let me see what I am missing and how I can make up for it."

- "There is absolutely no way this is going to work," can become, "I will give my best to make this work."

Surround Yourself With Positivity

Multiple studies have shown that you are or you become the average of five people you spend the most amount of time with. In order to become a more positive version of yourself, make sure you surround yourself with happy, positive people. Not only positivity contagious, but also you will learn different ways to convert negative to positive. Here are some nice tips to help you attract positive people.

Have self-belief - People interacting with you can sense if you have or don't have self-belief. If you lack self-belief, you are likely to attract others who also lack this crucial personality-boosting element. Self-belief starts with acknowledging and accepting who you are as you are. It is the first step towards improvement. Identify and acknowledge all your strengths as well as your vulnerabilities. When you have belief in yourself, then you can showcase your authentic self to the world without shame or guilt, and positive people are attracted to such honesty and openness.

Forgive freely - Holding on to anger and resentment is a sure way to enhance anxiety and stress in your life, which are bound to spill into your relationships as well. Not only this, but people can also easily sense the resentment you hold, and positive people will always back away from you.

Therefore, forgive the mistakes of everyone, including your own, and free yourself of burden. Remind yourself that everything in this world happens for a reason, and if someone hurt, intentionally or otherwise, then that too has a reason, the most obvious one being an important lesson for you to learn.

All of us stumble, make mistakes, and then find the courage to correct them and move on in life. This process is what helps us to grow and develop into better human beings. The lightness you experience after you forgive will make you so happy and relieved that positivity will bubble up inside you, and an increasing number of positive people will be attracted to you.

Harnessing the Power of Positivity

Positive attracts positive - Unlike in science where opposites attract, in psychology, like attracts like. If you are positive, then you will attract other positive people into your life. Embrace people who motivate and inspire you to achieve your best. Similarly, you must also contribute to other peoples' lives by being a source of motivation and inspiration for them.

Don't hesitate to celebrate others' success as much as your own. Surround yourself with people who believe in your dreams and will work with you to achieve them as much as you work with them to help them achieve theirs. This approach is the perfect recipe for a great romantic relationship too. Both of you should add value to each other's life even as you retain and be proud of your own individuality and identity.

If you are by default, a person who sees the glass half-empty, remember the change to become a positive-thinking person is going to take time. A bit of effort and persistence are needed from your end. However, remember that when the change happens, it will be really worth your while. It is highly rewarding to have a positive frame of mind at all times, even if the change is going to take some time. Your entire life will take on a new look, and your ability to handle love and romance will soar.

Chapter Seven

Importance of Communication in Relationships

The power and importance of communication between partners can never be undermined. Talking and bonding with your partner is one of the best ways to build intimacy and strength in a relationship. I was slowly but surely getting out of the cocoon I had built around myself, driven by anxiety and fear.

I was becoming increasingly confident about myself, even as I worked towards building my ability to accept and embrace my weaknesses and personal problems. With the help of a professional counselor, I had learned to come to terms with my attachment style and was continuously working on it to improve my chances of happiness and joy in relationships.

I had, in fact, reached out to my parents and spoken about their seeming lack of love and affection towards me. They were very upset and sad that I saw their behavior based on noble intentions in a different light. My dad told me, "My darling daughter, nothing in the world will replace you in our lives. If you are not happy, then all our hard work would go waste because we did everything for you."

My mom continued, "The reason why we had to work extra hard was that we had very limited means, and we wanted you to have the best money could buy. Therefore, both of us were so caught up in making money that we seem to have neglected your other needs. We love you, unconditionally, and your happiness is our only concern."

After a heart-to-heart conversation, my relationship with my parents was also improving, and I was gradually beginning to look at life with anticipation. Now, back to the story that tells you the importance of communication in a relationship.

One of my failed relationships (believe me when I tell you that I was smart enough to run a few thousand miles from this one) had a very funny experience for me. His name was Keifer (again name changed to ensure privacy), and he was an exceedingly quiet chap. He was a nice chap (or so I thought initially) but very, very silent. Getting even a few words out of him was difficult.

We were still in the dating phase, and I was a wee bit hesitant about taking this relationship to the next level. You know how you instinctively feel that something is wrong. But, you cannot really put your finger on what is causing the problem. Little by little, I made Keifer open up about himself.

I started by talking about myself. I told him about my problems with anxiety and how I dealt with my parents. I told him how much I love rock music.

I asked him, "Do you like music?"

He said, "Yes!"

I asked him, "What kind of music you like?" When you put such open-ended questions, you expect the conversation tone to be set for a long time because it is so easy to talk about what kind of music you like, right? But Keifer answered, "All kinds!" Then, complete silence followed.

Then, hoping to prod him on, I continued, "I love the feeling of the 80s rock music. I just need to listen to the opening notes of Bon Jovi's 'Living On A Prayer," and my heart simply lifts."

His reply to his highly enthusiastic statement was, "Oh! I see!" It was painful, initially. But he was a nice guy. Quiet and decent, I thought. So, I persisted in my efforts to slowly draw him out. I opened up my own life a lot more in the hope that he would also do the same.

Importance of Communication in Relationships

He was an amazing listener. I could talk for hours together, and he would listen without saying a single word. It made me feel so good that talking to him while he listened became a habit in all our meetings and interactions. I was still not ready to move to the next step in the relationship. It was nothing more than a few casual dates.

I urged him to talk openly without taboos, limits, or fears. I reassured him that what we speak to each other will not go beyond the two of us. Slowly he started opening up. He started talking about his past relationships so much that I began to wish I hadn't made such an effort to make him open up! He never seemed to stop talking, and I began to wish he would go back to his silent mode. He seemed better than now.

The details of his relationships got so sordid that I had to use an excuse for him not to go into so much detail. In fact, the sordidness got to me, and I suddenly realized that Keifer used his silence to hide his perversion. He knew that if he started talking, then any sensible woman would quickly gauge his true nature and would run away. So, he used the silent personality to appear wise and a man of few words.

I got the hang of him within very few words and, like any sensible woman, ran from him as far as I could. I told him we don't seem to be cut of the same cloth, and we shouldn't even try to start a relationship. I thank my good sense to have chosen to listen to and follow my initial instincts about this man and not taking the relationship to the next level.

There is no doubt that communication played an important role in helping me discover the true nature of Keifer. If I had chosen to accept his silence without protest or without trying to know more about him before committing myself to him, I would have been in deep trouble. Perhaps, my anxiety issues, which I had managed to keep at bay until now, would be returned with a vengeance resulting in irreparable damages to my heart and mind. I was able to avert such a disaster, thanks to my insistence of having an open, honest, and no-holds-barred communication channel between us.

Human beings are inherently social creatures, and we crave connection. In the absence of this human connection, we feel lonely, misunderstood, and isolated. This sense of connection plays a central role in improving our mental and emotional well-being and a sense of satisfaction. Interacting with people makes our life seem worth living. Try and remember

Importance of Communication in Relationships

a time when you felt lonely and miserable. Suppose during this time, if someone were to come and simply say a few words, a bit of the loneliness and misery would have definitely lessened.

Or think of another time when you were sick and alone at home. A good friend decided to stop by and say hello and ask about your health. Didn't you feel better already? At least during the period, your friend was with you, talking and chatting? Well, that is the power of communication. It automatically creates a connection. Just talking to someone else can make a big difference to our mental and emotional well-being.

Healthy communication is essential for a happy and meaningful relationship, and communication in a relationship should go deeper than small talk. While asking your partner how their day went is nice, it is not enough, especially if you want to keep anxiety and stress out of your relationship. Here are some ways in which communication plays an important part, not only in strengthening a relationship but also in reducing existing angst and anxiety felt by either or both partners.

How Does Effective Communication Impact Relationships?

Communication in a relationship goes far beyond mere information sharing. It helps partners create strong, unbreakable bonds with each other. These bonds are what sustain the relationship and make it meaningful and fulfilling. In the absence of any communication gaps, any relationship thrives.

Communication strengthens mutual respect - By default, human beings are empathetic. When we make the extra effort to communicate, which includes listening, then the purpose of empathy is served even better. When both partners take time to listen to what the other is saying, you are effectively giving yourselves the time needed to create mutual respect for each other's opinion.

Conversations between partners can lead to new insights as they brainstorm towards solutions for the same problem. After all, two heads are better than one. Moreover, such problem-solving episodes create increased bonding between the partners, enhancing intimacy and love.

Guesswork stays out of the relationship - When there is no lack of communication, there is nothing for either partner to guess. Neither partner will have

Importance of Communication in Relationships

to worry about reading the other's mind and also to worry if he or she is reading it right or not.

Moreover, an open, honest connection between the partners ensures there are no lies in the relationship. You don't have to worry about what to speak and what not to because you don't have to create stories based on earlier lies. You don't have to keep track of what you have withheld earlier. You don't have to worry about being 'found out.' All these elements ensure anxiety is kept at bay, and only loving and affectionate bonding happens. So, communication brings in trust and love and keeps out anxiety and worry.

How to Improve Communication in Relationships

Here are some excellent and simple suggestions as to how you can improve communication in your relationship.

First, identify the communication styles of you and your partner - Each of us has different communication styles. Remember, communication is not just about talking or saying words. It involves touch, writing, visual connection, and more. Moreover, communication is not only about sending messages correctly. It is also about receiving messages correctly.

You could say something according to your communication style, and your partner could receive something quite different because his or her communication style is quite different from yours. In order to ensure communication is effective, and messages are sent and received accurately between partners, the first step is to identify your own communication style.

One way of learning this is by watching for cues given by your partner as you communicate with him or her. For example, if you touch your partner, does he or she respond better than if you simply spoke from a distance? Is your partner more responsive to your gestures, or do your words get you a better response?

Also, suppose your communication style is predominantly auditory, which means to say you respond better with words. However, your partner might need more than words. For example, he or she responds better with touch (referred to as kinesthetic style). In such a case, simply saying "I love you" may not be enough. You might need to add a hug or kiss to these words for him or her to get the message across effectively and accurately.

Be honest and open - Two of the most important elements that play a vital role in improving

Importance of Communication in Relationships

communication in your relationship are honesty and openness. Speak only what you mean and ensure your verbal and nonverbal cues are in sync with each other. Don't hesitate to talk about your personal needs and desires.

Don't believe even for a single moment that by sacrificing your personal individuality, you are contributing positively towards the relationship. No, by holding back your true feelings and needs, you are jeopardizing the relationship because, unless your needs are met, you are not going to feel a sense of fulfillment and purpose in the relationship.

Don't avoid impending arguments and conflicts. Walking away when the situation is unpleasant to have a cooling period is fine. However, you must return to the topic when the nerves are calmed down and have an open discussion about what is nagging you.

Complete aversion to conflict means both you and your partner are burying negativity in the hope that it will go away. It won't! The only way negativity can be rooted out from the relationship is by talking about it objectively, wisely, maturely, and honestly.

Important Communication Skills to Master

Communication is a layered technique and consists of multiple components and skills, all of which need to be mastered if your ability to get the attention of, converse, and convince your partner. Some of the most important of these skills include the art of listening, nonverbal communication, straight-talking, and emotional control. Let us look at each of these in a bit of detail.

The art of listening - Communication has two parts, namely talking and listening. More often than not, when we talk about building communication skills, we only look at how to improve the way we talk. However, listening is an equally important skill to master to improve your communication skills.

Listening is not just about 'hearing' the words your partner is saying. It goes deeper. You must also try and understand your partner's underlying feelings and emotions. Trust is a natural outcome when your partner knows that you are really listening to his or her feelings and emotions and trying to solve problems.

Active listening creates an honest, secure environment for your relationship so that neither of you will ever be afraid to express your opinions, views, and ideas. The freedom from fear will enhance bonding between partners.

Nonverbal communication - A key aspect of listening is interpreting nonverbal cues emanating in the form of facial expressions, body posture, eye contact, gestures, and tone of voice, attitude, the way you breathe, and more. For example, suppose your partner says, "It's alright; I'll manage." But you see, the jaws are clenched, and he or she is not making eye contact with you. Now, you know the words don't really match with your partner's feelings. They are different. In such a situation, you need to dig deeper and find out if he or she can really 'manage.'

The reverse situation can also happen. Your partner says, "No, I will not entertain your boss and his wife in our home this weekend!" You are shocked at his or her words, and then you look at your partner's twinkling eyes, and you know he or she is merely pulling your leg.

Suppose you notice that in both of the above examples, the nonverbal cues were aligned with the speaker's true intentions. The words were only a cover, and in most cases, nonverbal cues present a more correct version of the speaker's state of mind than the verbal aspect of the conversation. Therefore, picking up nonverbal cues plays a crucial role in improving communication in your relationship.

Straight-talking - Avoid beating around the bush unnecessarily. Most often, straight-talking is the best form of communication. The more roundabouts you use, the more complex the conversations with your partner will be, and the higher the chances of misinterpretations and misunderstandings.

If you know that a conversation is going to be difficult, prepare for it. While it is true that you cannot be prepared for all kinds of potential responses, you can steel brace yourself for the worst and work backward during your prep. The skill of straight-talking requires a bit of dedicated practice and hard work. However, it is highly rewarding, and learning this critical communication skill is a worthy effort.

Emotional control - Your emotions play a crucial role in communication. These emotions impact your decision-making skills, affects your nonverbal cues, and how your partner interprets your messages. Most often, we allow our feelings to impact us without even being unaware of it.

From a relationship perspective, it is difficult to avoid emotions completely. After all, happiness and

Importance of Communication in Relationships

joy, the two most desired elements in a relationship, are powerful emotions that sustain the bond between you and your partner. Controlling emotions is not about ignoring them or suppressing them.

Emotion-control is about identifying, accepting, and embracing your emotions without getting trapped in their negative effects. It also involves learning to observe how emotions affect your partner. Being aware of emotions allows you to tweak your communication style so that messages are not colored by your feelings or those of your partner.

Effective communication plays a very important role in many areas of a relationship. It reflects what you mean to each other. It affects your mood, enhances love, decreases stress and anxiety, and ensures the bond between both of you remains strong and unbreakable.

Chapter Eight

Self-Esteem and Self-Confidence in Relationships

Considering that anxiety had ruled the better part of my life right from childhood, my self-confidence and self-esteem were at low levels. I would find it very difficult to make conversation on things that were not the common run-of-the-mill subjects. For example, I could talk with confidence about my favorite rock star and give details of how he or she makes notes and creates impeccable music.

However, if the subject under discussion was a bit complex, for example, finance and the world of money, then I would become mum! My lack of knowledge would become evident the minute I opened my mouth. I had been humiliated for this a couple of times when I was dating Alan, an investment banker.

Alan was a great guy and an even better investment banker. He was sharp and intelligent, and his colleagues and even his bosses looked up to him for help. His company analyses rarely failed, and people who followed his investment advice rarely lost money. In fact, most people chose to bet in favor of his advice. He was, of course, very proud of his accomplishments in his field, and he deserved all the accolades he got.

However, there was a small hitch in this regard. His pride bordered on vanity and arrogance, especially when it came to involving me in his talks of finance and money. He thought I was way beneath him and shouldn't make an effort to learn the subject because I would not be able to understand it at all.

One day, his humiliation reached abysmal depths. We were having a drink on a Friday evening with his investment banker friends. I was also there, sipping my drink and listening to the numerous jokes and banter involving a lot of jargon related to financial markets, stock markets, stock exchanges, and more. I was trying hard to grasp the meaning of their jokes because I wanted to be part of the group. I did not want to feel like an outsider. By the way, I was the only non-banker that day.

Suddenly I thought he could've told me not to come because I might feel out of place. But, I let that thought go. I was there and wanted to make all efforts to belong to the group. The entire group laughed loudly at all the jokes Alan cracked. One particular girl seemed to enjoy it the most, cracking up far more than the others did.

Of course, I didn't understand the jokes and remained silent with just a smile on my face, happy that the others were having fun even if I wasn't. Alan turned to me and asked, "What are you smiling for? You understood the joke or what?" The others, especially that girl, guffawed delightfully, although the laughter sounded cruel to my ears.

I said, "No, I didn't understand the joke. I was smiling, looking at all of you laughing."

He had a mocking smile on his face as he tried to explain to me what the joke was. What hurt me was Alan was treating me like a 13-year-old girl. He had a condescending attitude as he tried to make me understand. He was behaving like I had a learning disability. It was quite a humiliating experience for me.

My annoyance was even more pronounced when I saw that female colleague of his trying to suppress her giggles as I struggled to understand the joke. It was another colleague of Alan, Susan, who came to my help. Susan said, "C'mon, leave Amanda alone. It's not that finance and money are the only topics we can talk about. In fact, let's not talk shop and just focus on having fun today."

The others took a cue from her, and that unpleasant incident was forgotten, at least for that moment. However, the experience kept nagging me, and I needed to do something about it. I was happy at the way I was looking at the situation. In the earlier days, I would have simply gone home and cried myself to sleep. Today, instead of taking of route of self-pity, I decided to take control.

First things first. When I was alone with Alan, I told him I didn't like the way he treated me in front of his friends and colleagues. I told him I felt humiliated and hurt. Alan realized his mistake immediately and apologized for his behavior, saying he never meant to hurt me. It was only supposed to be a joke, and he was extremely sorry for hurting my feelings unintentionally.

Once this part was out of the way, I focused on the next part of my plan. I enrolled for an online beginner course in finances just to understand the basics. I knew that becoming a successful investment required more than just basic financial knowledge. But this was an attempt to learn something unfamiliar and new, which would build my self-confidence and self-esteem. Moreover, I really liked Alan, and I wanted to have conversations on the subject that he enjoyed. He had made a lot of effort to try and understand my love for rock music.

The course was a toughie for me, especially in the initial stages. I was not exceptionally good with finances and money. However, with time and effort, I realized that this subject wasn't really rocket science. The basics of finance was actually a lot of common sense. Personally, I learned the importance of financial prudence and how to handle my own money. Believe it or not, when I strictly adhered to the tips and suggestions given in the course on the subject of financial prudence that I was able to cut my personal monthly costs by nearly 25%, which went into savings.

I showed what I had done to Alan after the end of the course. He was not just thrilled with my efforts but also highly moved by it. He said, "I think you've unintentionally taught me a lesson on humility. I used to think that saving and investing money was something beyond an average person's intelligence. Today I know that my subject is nothing more than a bit of common sense combined with timely information, and of course, the willingness to work hard. Thank you, Amanda."

Self-Esteem and Self-Confidence in Relationships

It was my turn to be moved. I didn't expect this kind of reaction from Alan. I knew he was a nice guy and smart and intelligent too. But, he was also humble and sweet, accepting his mistakes with grace. I knew I found the right one. And I would do everything in my power to keep our relationship going.

However, the most important lesson for me from this experience was that developing self-confidence and self-esteem was essential for a happy, meaningful relationship.

Often, romantic relationships tend to change you as a person. Thanks to anxiety and fears associated with intimate relationships, it is possible that you choose to keep quiet about certain things and not talk about them with your partner. You may feel uncomfortable with the way your partner treats you at certain times. Yet, you choose not to do anything about it.

Numerous such 'silencing' of your thoughts can lead to suppression of feelings, which could accumulate into large unpleasant baggage. This is where self-confidence plays a big role. The more self-confident you are, the higher is your self-esteem, and the higher your chances of retaining your individuality in the relationships. Also, self-confidence and self-esteem are vital elements to keep out anxiety and worry about the value you bring to the relationship.

Importance of Self-Confidence in Relationships

Here are some great advantages of being a self-confident partner in a relationship.

Trust comes easily - The lack of self-confidence or low self-esteem is likely to make you insecure, which, in turn, makes you wary of your partner's true intentions when it comes to loving or caring for you. The worry about whether your partner really loves you or not is a key contributor to relationship anxiety.

Regardless of how much your partner says he or she cares for you, you will find it difficult to believe it because you lack self-worth. Thanks to your low self-esteem, you cannot trust what your partner says about you and your value. In such a situation, trust will not come easy. With high levels of self-confidence, it becomes easy to trust what your partner says about you because you know what he or she says is true.

You can save yourself from toxicity in relationships - One of the biggest pluses of being self-confident is that you believe you deserve the happiness you get. You can easily prevent yourself from falling for manipulative partners who can convince you that you don't deserve true love and happiness.

Self-confidence also helps you counter your own inner critic voice or at least tone down its negativity. With this attitude, you can stand up to people who try to put you down unnecessarily, thereby keeping toxicity from your life.

You will retain your individuality - Self-confidence gives you the power to be proud of who you are and what you represent. Regardless of the kind of people around you, you will retain your individuality and personality. Your need for others' opinions to value yourself will be considerably low, which means you will not be clingy and needy in a relationship, a trait that most partners value today. Moreover, if your partner has a bad influence on you, you will find the strength to counter it and walk away unscathed.

You will be a happy partner - Self-confidence empowers you to find happiness on your own, with or without a partner. A happy person can enhance the joy of any relationship. Moreover, you cannot share happiness with your partner if you are not happy with yourself.

After all, true happiness is being able to live your life according to your wishes and embracing and loving who you are, warts and all. A happy person always makes a better partner than a sad person. Your self-love will transfer onto your partner, too, and he or she will feel loved and wanted.

You will be free of the fear of intimacy - The lack of or low levels of self-confidence leads to feelings of insecurity which, in turn, makes you feel squeamish during intimate interactions, especially sex. When you have low levels of self-confidence, you will be anxious and worried about how you look and what your partner thinks about your body, skin color, etc.

When you make an effort to improve your self-confidence, you will feel sexy about yourself regardless of your external looks and profile. Being sexy has little to do with outside beauty and more to do with how you feel inside of yourself. Your self-confidence makes you love yourself for who you are and how you are made naturally. This feeling of self-confidence will shine through, and your partner will definitely find you attractive and sexy. And your fear of intimacy will disappear.

You will not over-analyze and overthink anything - Overthinking and overanalyzing are signs of relationship anxiety. With self-confidence, this kind of unrealistic and unnecessary overthinking will cease to happen. For example, if your partner has not responded to your text message, then you will not fret too much over it if your confidence levels are high. It is easy to convince yourself that he or she must be busy and will respond whenever possible.

Also, even if something was amiss and there is a big chance of your partner leaving you for any reason, your self-confidence will take care of you because you will find a way to be happy with or without your partner.

Therefore, it makes a lot of sense to invest time and energy to build up your self-confidence so that your romantic relationships are fulfilling, meaningful, and add value to your life as well as that of your partner.

Build Self-Confidence

It is time to remind yourself that self-confidence is not a genetic trait. It can be learned and imbibed into your psyche so deeply that it will become part of your personality. If you believe you are not smart, competent, or good enough to deserve the good things in life, then this belief can be changed.

You can become worthy and deserving of all the good things of life, regardless of what others think of you. The answer lies within you. The answer lies in building your self-confidence. Here are some ideas using which you can slowly but surely develop your self-confidence and bring it up to desirable, which, in turn, will attract positive changes in your life.

Groom yourself - While external looks may not be the ultimate element to build self-confidence, it is a great place to start the journey. Groom yourself to look good by making sure you have good, clean, and well-tailored clothes to wear. Silly as it may sound, ensure you shower every day using a nice-smelling soap or shower gel.

Dress well. This doesn't mean you have to buy expensive and designer clothes. If you dress well, your self-esteem gets a boost, giving you the mental energy needed to tackle the challenges in your world. A good physical profile is the first step to becoming more confident than now.

Grooming yourself includes learning how to talk clearly and slowly. This approach renders an image of a confident person so that when you talk, people listen to you. Similarly, the way you carry yourself is important. Stand tall and confident. Don't slouch when you sit. Throw your shoulders back and exude confidence through your posture.

Build self-awareness - Have you heard of how generals and commanders win battles? Their first strategy is to get to know as much as they can about their enemy and then work around weaknesses and vulnerabilities. When you are trying to build self-confidence, your biggest enemy would be yourself.

So, start your battle of self-confidence with building self-awareness. Know yourself well. Be conscious of how your thoughts come and go. Be aware of how you analyze things and situations. Get to know your strengths and weaknesses. Work on improving your strengths and eliminating your weaknesses or using them effectively as another form of strength.

Focus on your limitations. Are these limitations authentic, or have you created them based on prior experiences? Are you willing to do what it takes to breach these limits and achieve more than what you have done until now? The more questions you ask yourself, the more your self-awareness will rise.

Another highly useful element you have to learn about yourself is your core values and principles. What are the things that are important? Success? Career? Money? A great relationship? Family? Or something else? Spend some time with yourself and look deep within you and discover your values and principles. It makes sense to have not more than five elements on your core value list in order of preference.

This list then becomes your guide to how you should live your life. What kind of people should you allow into your life? What kind of career suits you so that these principles intact? When you live by the value and principles of your own, then you live an authentic life being true to yourself. And an authentic life is a great way to boost self-confidence.

Visualize yourself as being confident - How we think of ourselves and the image we create of ourselves in our mind plays a big role in self-confidence. Take the example of having a difficult conversation with your partner. Suppose you visualize yourself talking in a feeble voice, stumbling to say what you want to say at every step, your self-confidence is likely to take a beating.

On the contrary, visualize talking to your partner with confidence. Imagine yourself saying what you want to say confidently without stumbling. Visualize a confident posture of yourself as you look at your partner in the eye and tell him your problems. This kind of visualization technique helps to build your self-confidence and has the power to become a self-fulfilling prophecy.

Self-Esteem and Self-Confidence in Relationships

Be kind, compassionate, and generous - Being kind, compassionate, and generous is a great way of improving your self-image. People who have experienced these great qualities of yours are bound to say nice things about you, which are effective confidence boosters. Even if they don't say the nice things, you will feel good for showing kindness and compassion, which also is a great confidence booster.

When you think and believe you are a good person, this feeling and thought do great things to your self-confidence. So, don't hesitate to be kind and generous. Generosity doesn't have to come in the form of money and wealth alone. Giving your time to people is one of the best ways of making others happy.

Prepare for everything you do - When you do anything to the best of your abilities, your self-confidence gets a big boost. And the only way you can do your best is to prepare for it. No matter what you do, make sure you spend time and energy to prepare for it.

It could be something as simple as a surprise dinner date with your partner. Even for something as seemingly easy as this, you need to prepare well for the event to turn out as good as it deserves to turn out. You have to plan the date, time, venue, etc. What will be the surprise element? How do you plan to make it a surprise? There is so much to do that, without proper preparation, the dinner date might not turn out to a pleasant surprise at all.

If preparing for a simple dinner date requires so much thought and work, you can imagine how much more work is needed for other things. Therefore, we always work on preparation for almost everything you do. It might seem cumbersome in the initial stages. However, with time and practice, you will see that prep work becomes part of your regimen so much so that your daily to-do list will include the prep elements for the tasks of the day.

When you put in hard work and commitment, can success be far behind? And with every success comes a huge boost to your self-confidence and self-esteem.

Build as many skills as you can - Competence and skills are great confidence boosters. When you do something well, or you are highly skilled at something, then people are likely to reach out to you when your skills are required. Therefore, build as many skills as you can and become increase your knowledge and competence in your core skills.

For example, if you want to become a writer, invest time and energy to build and improve your writing skills. Make sure you allocate time every day to work on your writing. The more you invest resources in building this skill, the better you will write. In the same way, invest resources and learn new skills as well as improve your existing skills.

Replace a bad habit with a good one - Bad habits tend to dent our self-confidence, and good habits have a way of boosting our self-esteem. Therefore, a great way to enhance your self-confidence is to replace a bad habit with a good one. Start with something small. Here is a little example that can be achieved by most people.

What happens during your lunch break? Typically, you would finish your lunch and then end up chitchatting with your colleagues, right? Now, make a small change in this routine. Finish your lunch and replace the activity of chitchatting with your colleagues with a 30-minute walk. A park nearby would be great. However, if you don't have access to a park, then you can walk around your office block.

A simple start like this can do wonders for your self-confidence. Changing small habits at a time makes you realize that it is not difficult to take control of your life. You just need to take one little step at a time.

Do something that you have been putting off - Putting off or procrastinating makes you feel unworthy. You think to yourself, "I can't even do this small thing. What can I deserve?" You can imagine what these negative thoughts will do to your self-confidence, right?

Well, change the situation. Take up one activity that you have been putting off and do it right now. The feel-good hormones released at the end of completing the activity will keep you going for a while. Before these hormones get out of your system, do another such activity, and replenish your body again. Repeat this until procrastination is out of your life. You will see the huge uptake your self-confidence gets if you diligently implement this suggestion.

And finally, reread the chapter on positive thinking and how to deal with your inner critic voice and implement the ideas given there to replace your negative thoughts with positivity and happy thoughts. Self-confidence is like a pillar of support you build for yourself and for your use only. The stronger this pillar gets, the stronger you become. And the stronger you become, the better your relationships will be.

Conclusion

Romantic and intimate relationships act as a mirror. They reflect our inner personality. They can soothe us as much as they can inflame our emotions. When the relationship is 'right,' our life becomes magical. Getting your relationship right is in your hands. If you give in your anxiety and fears, then the magic is lost and the connection between you and your partner breaks.

Relationships are successful only in the presence of truckloads of patience, vulnerability, tenderness, and trust. The problem is that anxiety has the power to erode and eat into these vital elements of a great relationship. It is imperative, therefore, to keep anxiety at bay so that your relationship gets filled with romance and love.

It makes sense to end this book by identifying and understanding the elements that make a secure and strong relationship. So let's get started.

Trust - Trust is an essential component of a great relationship. If partners don't or can't trust each other, then that relationship is bound to create anxiety for both of you. And trust is not just about cheating but also in other aspects of life. Both partners must be able to trust each other that promises will be kept. Trust is about knowing that both partners have each other's back in times of need. And they are there for each other for both small as well as big things in life.

Intimacy - Emotional and physical intimacy is a done thing for any relationship to flourish. Don't hold back about letting your partner know that you find him or her attractive. Let your partner know that you enjoy intimate time spent with him or her. This kind of honesty helps to boost each other's self-esteem.

It is common for partners in long-term relationships to put physical intimacy in the back burner, thanks to multiple other distractions like children, family, etc. It is vital that both of you bring back the intimacy in your relationship if you want it to flourish.

Use opportunities to get away from work and children and spend some we-time together. Go on a date again. Take a short holiday. If time is a problem, just watching a movie together can be a great way to enhance intimacy.

Communication - If you and your partner cannot talk openly and honestly with each other, there is no

Conclusion

way your relationship will last, forget flourishing. In fact, many couples are so tired of all the nagging and fighting that they tend to stop communicating with each other in the hope of putting an end to all the nagging, a bad approach for any relationship.

It is imperative that you and your partner talk and communicate with each other. Listen when your partner is talking and teach him or her to listen when you are talking. Learn the art of communication because it is a crucial element in a successful relationship.

And thanks to advanced technology, you are a variety of communication options. A simple text message is saying, "I am stuck at work. I will be late. I am truly sorry for this," can do wonders to calm each other's frayed nerves and keep worries and anxiety at bay.

A simple, 'I am really sorry, I forgot about the laundry. I should have been more attentive," can get rid of anger and resentment in a jiffy. Avoid holding back information from each other.

A good sense of humor - All relationships have their bad and good moments. Being able to look back at the bad times and to laugh together is a great way to build deep connections and trust with each other.

Partners who don't take life very seriously tend to be less bothered about anxiety and worry.

Laughing together is also a great way to build emotional intimacy. Do something together that will bring out the laughs as often as you can. Even the simple activity of watching a comedy show that both of you like is good enough for this.

Have common goals and interests - Sharing goals and interests is a wonderful way to strengthen bonds between partners in a relationship. Couples are known to thrive when they share common goals and interests and work in tandem to achieve these goals. Having the support of your partner to achieve your individual goals is great, of course. However, sharing goals and reaching goal posts together is even better.

Sharing goals can be in any form. It could be something like saving money for an exotic holiday and or working on a fitness regime to run a marathon together. Common goals are excellent bond creators.

Daily exchanges of love and affection - Again, this can be in simple ways. A simple 'I love you' message in his or her lunch box or through a personal messaging system like Whatsapp or SMS could be enough to make your partner feel secure and happy.

Conclusion

Make time for each other regularly - As the relationship deepens, chances of you and your partner taking each other for granted are high. Be conscious of this and ensure that you make time for each other regularly. It need not be an exotic vacation or something big. It can be something as simple as having dinner together at least once a week minus children, work, or any other distractions.

Respect each other's boundaries - While it is great to have common goals and interests, it is equally important to respect each other's boundaries. Each of you must have an individuality of your own that is strong and powerful. Only then will you feel secure and happy as a twosome. Else, a sense of codependency will creep in, leaving in its trail feelings of anxiety and insecurity.

If your partner needs time alone to complete an important project that will get him or her a raise at the workplace, give him or her the time and space for it. When your partner achieves his or her dreams, share their happiness. Avoid comparing your goals with those of your partner's. While your partner is following his or her dream, work on your dream too.

And finally, give each other a sense of belonging in the relationship. At the end of a hectic day, when both of you return home, you should feel that you have come home to love and affection. You and your partner together make the relationship. If either of you is missing, then the relationship does not exist. So, do everything in your power to treat each other as an important member of the partnership!

If you work with all the ideas and tips given in this book one at a time, relationship anxiety will show itself out of you and your relationship. Use the suggestions wisely and turn over a new leaf. Discover the new YOU and find the power of love and romance in a fulfilling, meaningful relationship.

References

https://www.psychalive.org/how-to-deal-with-relationship-anxiety/

https://www.goodtherapy.org/blog/how-anxiety-destroys-relationships-and-how-to-stop-it-0622155

https://www.psychologytoday.com/us/therapists/astrid-robertson-olympia-wa/169991

https://www.healthline.com/health/relationship-anxiety#signs

https://wanderamylessly.com/home/2019/4/24/working-through-relationship-anxiety

https://www.psychologytoday.com/us/blog/women-s-mental-health-matters/201509/7-ways-deal-negative-thoughts

https://psychcentral.com/blog/8-healthy-ways-to-deal-with-jealousy/

https://psychcentral.com/blog/why-healthy-relationships-always-have-boundaries-how-to-set-boundaries-in-yours/

https://www.williamstrachanfamilylaw.com/2015/02/conflict-good-relationship/

https://www.psychologytoday.com/us/blog/close-encounters/201704/10-tips-solving-relationship-conflicts

https://www.psychologytoday.com/us/blog/living-forward/201609/four-ways-stop-feeling-insecure-in-your-relationships

https://greatergood.berkeley.edu/article/item/ten_ways_to_become_more_grateful1

https://psychcentral.com/blog/what-self-care-is-and-what-it-isnt-2/#:~:text=Self%2Dcare%20is%20any%20activity,improved%20mood%20and%20reduced%20anxiety.

https://www.mayoclinic.org/healthy-lifestyle/stress-management/in-depth/positive-thinking/art-20043950

https://www.capitalfm.co.ke/lifestyle/2018/04/05/10-essential-elements-of-a-strong-relationship/2/

https://www.psychologytoday.com/us/blog/compassion-matters/201307/how-your-attachment-style-impacts-your-relationship

https://www.bridestory.com/blog/6-reasons-why-you-should-have-self-confidence-in-a relationship#:~:text=When%20your%20self%2Dconfidence%20is,partner's%20intentions%20in%20loving%20you.&text=When%20you%20have%20self%2Dconfidence,that%20your%20partner%20loves%20you.

https://blog.mindvalley.com/the-power-of-positive-thinking/

https://www.healthline.com/health/cognitive-distortions#emotional-reasoning

References

https://zenhabits.net/25-killer-actions-to-boost-your-self-confidence/

https://www.verywellmind.com/attachment-styles-2795344

https://www.tonyrobbins.com/ultimate-relationship-guide/key-communication-relationships/

https://blog.smarp.com/top-5-communication-skills-and-how-to-improve-them

CPSIA information can be obtained
at www.ICGtesting.com
Printed in the USA
BVHW040827191120
593711BV00006B/272